Sam Murphy

GET FIT Walking

A & C Black
London

Acknowledgements

With thanks to YMCA Fitness Industry Training, for allowing me access to their walking for fitness instructors' course, to Sarah Connors from Back on Track physiohterapy for ensuring my biomechanics and anatomy were up to speed, and to Ian Logan for valuable feedback on the overall text.

Published in 2006 by A & C Black Publisher Ltd
38 Soho Square, London W1D 3HB
www.acblack.com

Copyright © 2006 Sam Murphy

ISBN 0 7136 6460 6

A CIP catalogue record for this book is available from the British Library.

Note: While every effort has been made to ensure that the content of this book is as technically accurate and as sound as possible, neither the authors nor the publishers can accept responsibility for any injury or loss sustained as a result of the use of this material.

Acknowledgements
Cover photograph © Royalty-Free /Corbis
Cover and inside design by James Watson
Printed and bound in Dubai by Oriental Press

Contents

Introduction

Walking. It is one of the most natural activities known to humankind – it's simple, practical and beneficial to mind and body. It can help you switch off from day-to-day stresses and problems, or give you the time and space to solve them. It can entail striding out alone on challenging terrain, or socialising with others on a weekend ramble. But can it be used to improve and maintain fitness? Can it assist in weight loss, and make significant changes to our health? You bet it can. As a runner, I had always thought of walking as simply a way of getting from A to B – not as a fitness activity. But nine months of injury forced me to resort to walking, and I can tell you, I was surprised at just how challenging – and effective – it could be. Although my injury problems are in the past, and running remains my first love, I still use walking as part of my all-round fitness regime – not just because it gives my joints a break but because I simply enjoy it so much. It's great to see my favourite running routes at a pace at which I can actually take in the scenery!

In an age where everything is high-tech, fast and sophisticated, walking may seem a little tame and, well, basic, to stand up as a bona fide exercise activity, but study after study shows that walkers reap many of the benefits that people who engage in far more vigorous activities enjoy, with a lower risk of injury, a higher level of adherence and more opportunities to fit their activity into a busy day.

That said, strolling along the street at a snail's pace, or walking with poor technique, won't help you get the most from your fitness activity. You need some know-how to plan a walking programme to boost your fitness or shed pounds, to protect your heart and joints or even to enhance your well-being – mental and physical. And that's where this book comes in. By drawing on the latest scientific research and translating it into usable information, *Get Fit Walking* will show you how to make every step count, whether you want to walk away from excess weight, safeguard your health, travel on foot from Land's End to John O'Groats, or simply get a little more active. You'll find all the information you need about how much walking you need to do, what sort of pace you need to walk at, what to wear, how to set goals and stay motivated, and how to ensure you stay injury-free. The great thing about walking is that *anyone* can do it – it doesn't matter if you are 65 years old, 10 kg overweight or pregnant with your first child. You can – and will – benefit from making walking for fitness part of your life. Ready? Then walk this way...

Best foot forward

The human body – a complex and highly versatile construction that any engineer would be proud of – was designed for movement. But the fact is, most of us don't move for long enough, or often enough, to keep ourselves in good health. The British Heart Foundation (BHF) reports that 68 per cent of us in the UK don't take enough exercise to achieve health benefits, not to mention lose excess weight or improve fitness. Other research shows that over the past 50 years, the amount of energy adults aged 20–60 expend per day has dropped by 500 calories.

Yet the BHF's National Centre for Physical Activity and Health estimates that 37 per cent of coronary heart disease (CHD) deaths are related to inactivity, and would therefore be easily preventable if we were only to get a little more active.

One solution is to go and join a gym – work out for 45 minutes, three times a week and spend the rest of the week with your bottom firmly ensconced on the sofa. But research shows that more than half of the people who adopt this approach have given up their fitness regime within six months (and on average members only use the gym once a week). So why not choose an activity that is *already* part of your daily life?

The case for getting fit on your own two feet

Walking is the most natural form of human movement. We don't have to master any new skills to do it, as we already do it every day (although usually not as much as we should), and it is easy to fit into any lifestyle.

I'm not suggesting that you won't benefit from working out in a gym – or swimming, or playing tennis – but with these activities, you have to rely on other people, or travel to a particular destination, between particular hours, and perhaps have to wait to use the equipment or facilities that you want. With walking, on the other hand, you simply need to open the front door and go.

You can go on your own, with your dog, your partner, a friend or a group. You can go first thing, when the world is just waking up, in the evening, to help shake off the stresses of the day... you can go to the countryside and take in the scenery and fresh air on a day hike, or perhaps make it a purposeful daily journey, by commuting to work on foot. And since you don't need to get changed into specialist equipment to walk (except for some good supportive shoes), you can even go when you have a spare 10 minutes – something you can't really do with running, swimming or the gym. The unique versatility of walking makes it accessible and achievable for anyone.

> Walking is cheap and easy to do. No matter where I am, I can always find time to walk.
>
> *Claire, from London*

Running and walking – head to head!

Running is a great form of exercise – and, really, just an extension of walking. But for many, running is too challenging an activity to begin with, and taking it up results in discomfort and disillusionment, and, inevitably, giving up. I certainly advocate running, but if you are taking your first steps on the road to fitness, I recommend that you, er, don't run before you can walk!

Muscling in

Walking and running are both mainly focused on the lower body. But walking works the 'back' of the body, i.e. the calves and hamstrings, more than running to propel the body forward. Running uses much more of the front of the thighs, as the knee is bent more deeply when the foot is on the ground than in walking.

Counting calories

There isn't an enormous amount of difference in the calorie expenditure for walking or running a mile – a study in the journal *Medicine & Science in Sports & Exercise* in 2004 found that the average energy expenditure for running 1 mile was 113 calories, while the average for walking it was 81 calories. But of course, you'll cover a mile more quickly if you run. A 10-stone woman burns 318 calories walking for an hour – that doubles to 635 if she runs at a 10-minute mile pace. But it also reaches almost 400 calories per hour if she walks uphill, and goes still higher if she is racewalking.

Shock factor

In walking, a force equal to 4.5 times your body weight is exerted through the heel. That's why flip-flops aren't good walking attire! But in running, this rises to 9 times the body weight. For anyone with existing joint problems, a less than optimal level of fitness or for someone returning to exercise after a long break, walking is more forgiving on the body than running. And as you get fitter, you can think about adding some walk-run sessions to your weekly workouts.

Why walking is medicine for your body, mind and spirit

If you're not convinced that walking will reap the health and fitness benefits that you want to achieve, read on for some compelling evidence.

Walk away from heart disease

Walking for 30 minutes a day is enough to produce significant heart health benefits, says *The Physician and Sportsmedicine* journal. In the large-scale Nurses' Health Study, women who walked briskly (in the study, brisk was defined as a fairly unchallenging 3–4 mph pace) for at least 3 hours per week had the same amount of protection against heart disease as women who exercise vigorously for an hour and a half a week – both groups were 30–40 per cent less likely to develop heart disease than their sedentary counterparts. As for the guys, well, a study of over 44,000 men in the United States revealed an 18 per cent reduction in heart disease risk with half an hour of brisk walking each day. The BHF's National Centre for Physical Activity and Health says that 9 per cent of deaths from CHD in the UK could be avoided if people who are currently sedentary, or only sporadically active, increased their activity to a moderate level.

Walk off excess pounds!

Research suggests that nearly 30 per cent of men and nearly 45 per cent of women are trying to lose weight at any given time. Walking presents a convenient, accessible and effective strategy. Given that women tend to gain a pound a year from 37 to 64, the role of regular walking in increasing calorie expenditure is very important. Walking for one hour at 4 mph burns nearly 300 calories (based on a 70 kg person). Walking up stairs burns nearly 300 calories in *half* an hour. But it isn't just through burning more calories that walking can help assist weight loss. It teaches your body to mobilise fat more efficiently, releasing it from 'adipose' tissue where it is stored and metabolising it (burning it for energy). It also enhances the development of the enzymes needed to break down fats to release energy. So the fitter you are, the more efficient the fat-burning process. Incidentally, in a large-scale epidemiological study, people who quit smoking but remained sedentary gained 5 lb in a two-year period. Regular physical activity after stopping smoking prevented this weight gain.

Walk your bones and joints stronger

Walking is weight-bearing exercise – so it is good for your bones – but it is low impact, so it's good for your joints, too. Like muscle, bone responds to the amount of stress it is placed under. If your average demand is to get up every hour to fetch another beer from the fridge, your bones won't be as strong as if your routine involves weekly football or aerobics. A strikingly clear example of the effect exercise has on bone is how the 'playing' arm of a tennis player reveals a significantly greater bone density than that of their less active arm.

You can't begin to exercise for bone health soon enough, as the integrity of bone begins to decline from as young as 30 – and in women, this deterioration accelerates rapidly after the menopause (read more on pages 111–12). But that doesn't mean that it's ever too late to begin. While improvements to bone density are modest in later life, activity does slow further decline, which is essential in reducing the risk of osteoporosis. The best type of exercise for bone is described as 'bone-loading' or 'weight-bearing' exercise. This is one instance where something with more joint impact, like jogging, is more beneficial than walking. But the evidence about bone health and walking is mixed. As far as the rest of the connective tissues go, however, there is no doubt that moderate exercise like walking strengthens the ligaments and tendons and nourishes cartilage, protecting against arthritis and other age and inactivity-related joint deterioration. Walking is also one of the best forms of exercise for preventing or alleviating back pain.

Walk your way to sanity!

Being physically fit is associated with mental well-being, including positive mood, reduced anxiety and being less depressed. Whether that is because mentally healthy people have a greater tendency to be active, or whether people who are active gain some kind of immunity against mental ill-health has not been proven categorically. But given that activity has been successfully prescribed to treat anxiety and mild depression, throw in its myriad physical benefits and I'd say it's not worth waiting to find out! What's more, a study by the mental health charity MIND found that more than 50 per cent of people felt physical exercise was at least as effective – if not more so – as drug therapy in dealing with depression.

Research from the University of Indiana showed that walking for 20 minutes or more gave a significant boost to mental health. In fact, it showed that, done regularly, it had the same positive outcome as a course of psychotherapy. It seems that more frequent workouts, over a long-term period, are most effective. Another reason to favour walking over stop-start gym routines.

> There is something immensely satisfying about getting around on your own two feet – you have a real sense if independence
>
> *Margaret, from Worthing*

Walk away from stress

Walking is a great way of getting rid of pent-up stress. While stress – and its physiological manifestation – is a necessary and important function, the 21st century lifestyle doesn't allow us to fight or flee from stressful situations. No, we just sit there and stew or simmer! The hormones that are released in stressful times, such as cortisol and adrenaline, therefore do not get a chance to dissipate and simply circulate in the blood, while blood pressure and heart rate soar. One of the effects of adrenaline is to make the blood clot faster (this would be good in a 'fight' situation, where you may be injured). But in the office or hectic home, the resulting 'thicker' blood has a far more serious implication: that of increasing heart attack or stroke risk. The good news, though, is that research shows that regular moderate activity reduces this tendency to form blood clots, and has a relaxing and calming effect on the body and mind. Research from

Texas A&M University also found that physically fit subjects in a study were better able to cope with unexpected physical and mental challenges than unfit subjects. The better shape you are in, the more able your body is to handle stress, concluded the researchers.

Walk for a longer life

Three major studies have found that, regardless of weight, active women live longer than sedentary women. In a 16-year period of study, women who were active for at least 4 hours a week were 30 per cent less likely to die than women who did less than 1 hour per week. In another study, which looked at more than 10,000 men, all-cause death rate was almost three times higher for sedentary men.

I hope you are now convinced that walking is a well-trodden route to better health and fitness. Throughout the book, you will find *Let's walk* panels, with yet more reasons to step out. So read on to find out how to get the most out of your fitness walking.

What will happen when you become a regular walker

Get it right and you can expect the following positive changes to your body.

- Less body fat and greater efficiency to burn fat
- Greater muscle tone in the hips, thighs, calves and bottom
- Less risk of back pain
- Fewer aches and pains due to increased mobility
- Improved circulation and better digestion
- Greater resilience to stress and less anxiety and depression
- Improved cholesterol profile and better control of insulin
- A heart that can pump out more blood with every beat
- Improved sleep
- Fewer colds and other infections
- Stronger respiratory system, so you can take in or expel more air with fewer breaths
- Enhanced posture.

Getting started

Walking is already familiar territory to the musculoskeletal system (the muscles and bones), but increasing your speed to a pace that will have a beneficial effect on your fitness will undoubtedly demand more cardiovascular strength and endurance than ambling around the shops. That's not to say you need to be fit to start with, as regular walking will begin to trigger these changes almost immediately, but it's wise to go through the fitness checklist below to determine whether you should seek medical advice, or see a physiotherapist, before you embark on a walking for fitness programme.

Bear in mind, though, however inactive you are currently, the words of lauded Swedish exercise scientist Dr Per Astrand. 'A medical examination is more urgent for those who plan to remain inactive than for those who intend to get into good physical shape!'

> Walking in London had made me see so many more places than if I was stuck on a bus or tube. I really feels as if I am part of the city.
>
> *Gemma, from London*

Testing times

Take the following measurements and tests below to give yourself a snapshot of your current health and fitness. This will also give you a 'baseline' from which to work on improvements.

Body Mass Index (BMI)

BMI is a simple way of assessing your body weight status. It's not infallible, as it does not distinguish between fat and muscle, but it does allow you to get an idea of whether you are a healthy weight and is a useful guideline if you

What it means

Underweight	under 20
Normal weight	20 – 24.9
Overweight	25 – 29.9
Very overweight	30+

Fitness checklist

Answer the questions below carefully to see whether a medical examination or testing is advisable.

■ Has your doctor ever said that you have a heart condition?

■ Do you feel pain in your chest when you do physical activity?

■ In the past month, have you had chest pain when you were not doing physical activity?

■ Do you lose your balance because of dizziness, or do you ever lose consciousness?

■ Do you have a bone or joint problem (such as osteoarthritis or osteoporosis) or an injury that could be made worse by a change in your physical activity?

■ Are you currently taking medication for high blood pressure or a heart condition or is your blood pressure higher than 160/90?

■ Are you pregnant or have you recently had a baby?

■ Are you significantly overweight? This equates to a BMI > 30 (see below).

■ Do you have a parent, brother or sister who has or had premature heart disease (in men under 55 or women under 65)?

■ Do you believe there are any other reasons why fitness walking may pose a threat to your health or wellbeing?

If you answered 'yes' to any of the above questions, see your doctor before you embark on a fitness walking regime or continue with your existing exercise regime. In addition, if you are a woman over 55, a man over 45, or have been completely sedentary for more than a year, it is wise to check with your doctor before beginning.

don't have access to a body fat assessment.

Measure your height in metres and your weight in kilos, and then divide your weight by your height squared:

$W/H^2 = BMI$

Resting heart rate

Your resting heart rate (RHR) represents the number of times your heart beats each minute when you are at rest, to pump blood around the body. Since a strong cardiovascular system allows your heart to pump more blood with every beat, your resting heart rate will drop as you get fitter, so it is a useful marker of your progress.

Measure your heart rate before you even get out of bed or eat or drink anything. Breathe evenly and normally and place two fingers (not your thumb) on the thumb-side of your inner wrist. Count the number of beats you feel in 60 seconds, counting the first beat as '0'. Repeat the test, add the results of both tests together and divide by 2 for the most accurate reading.

What it means

60 or below	good cardiovascular fitness
60–80	average (women tend to have slightly higher RHR than men)
80–100	high but still considered acceptable
100+	abnormally high, indicating poor cardiovascular fitness or a medical problem

Do bear in mind, however, that an abnormally low or high resting heart rate is not always indicative of a problem with cardiovascular fitness – it could be just an innate idiosyncrasy. Highly trained endurance athletes, such as Tour de France cyclists, have recorded resting heart rates in the late 20s and early 30s, while a normal, active person could have an RHR as high as 90 bpm without any accompanying health problems. Also note that if you are unwell or exhausted, your resting heart rate will be higher than normal.

Aerobic fitness – the Rockport Mile Walking Test

The well-established Rockport Test is a way of testing your aerobic fitness. The result is an estimate of your maximal oxygen uptake (known as your VO^2 max), which is the amount of oxygen your body can take in and utilise each minute.

Measure or mark out a flat, obstacle-free course of 1 mile (1609 metres, or 4 laps of a standard athletics track). Warm up (see pages 31–3 for how to do it properly) and then walk the course as fast as you can, recording your time with a stopwatch. Immediately on finishing, record your heart rate for 1 minute (as described above in resting heart rate). Now get a calculator and feed your results into the following equation and it will calculate your VO^2 max for you, or go to http://www.brian-mac.demon.co.uk/rockport.htm to save you doing the maths.

133 – (0.07 x your weight in lbs) – (0.38 x your age in years) + (6.3 x 1 (for males) or 0 (for females)) – (3.26 x time walk took in minutes) – (0.1565 x heart rate (BPM))

Example: You are a 30-year old female who weighs 130 lbs. You took 12 minutes to walk the course and your heart rate at the end was 135bpm.

133 – (0.07 x 130) – (0.38 x 30) + 0 – (3.26 x 12) – (0.1565 x 135)
133 –   9.1   –   11.4   + 0 –   39.12   –   21.12
= 52.26 ml/kg/min (the measurement is how many ml of blood are utilised, per kilogram of your body weight, per minute).

Now compare your result to the values below:

FEMALE

AGE	VERY POOR	POOR	FAIR	GOOD	VERY GOOD	EXCELLENT
20–29	<23.6	23.6–28.9	29–32.9	33–36.9	37–41	>41
30–39	<22.8	22.8–26.9	27–31.4	31.5–35.6	35.7–40	>40
40–49	<21	21–24.4	24.5–28.9	29–32.8	32.9–36.9	>36.9
50–59	<20.2	20.2–22.7	22.8–26.9	27–31.4	31.5–35.7	>35.7
60+	<17.5	17.5–20.1	20.2–24.4	24.5–30.2	30.3–31.4	>31.4

			MALE			
AGE	VERY POOR	POOR	FAIR	GOOD	VERY GOOD	EXCELLENT
20–29	<33	33–36.4	36.5–42.4	42.5–46.4	46.5–52.4	>52.4
30–39	<31.5	31.5–35.4	35.5–40.9	41–44.9	45–49.4	>49.4
40–49	<30.2	30.2–33.5	33.6–38.9	39–43.7	43.8–48	>48
50–59	<26.1	26.1–30.9	31–35.7	35.8–40.9	41–45.3	>45.3
60+	<20.5	20.5–26	26.1–32.2	32.3–36.4	36.5–44.2	>44.2

Activity level

How many steps do you take on an average day? You may have heard about the '10,000 steps per day' recommendation – a conclusion drawn recently by some health authorities that to achieve fitness benefits, you need to take 10,000 steps per day. Well, if you are like the majority of the population of the Western world, you walk significantly less than that. According to a recent report in the journal *Sports Medicine*, fewer than 5000 steps are typical of today's sedentary lifestyle. American researchers asked 1000 people to wear a pedometer from the moment they got up until bed time – the average American woman aged 18–59 took between 4500–5500 steps – slightly less than men of the same age.

The best way to find out how many steps you are taking is to clip on a pedometer as soon as you are up and about, and wear it all day, then take note of your baseline figure. The result may come as a rude awakening!

Below 4500	Very inactive (equates to half an hour of walking or less in total per day)
4500–6000	Average sedentary person
6000–8000	Above average (equates to roughly an hour of walking in total per day)
7500–8000	Active
8000–10,000	Very active
10,000–12,500	Highly active

There's nothing like progress

With all the above tests and trials, you will find that after a few weeks of regular walking, your results will improve. So it's a good idea to make a note of how you fared now, and then repeat the tests in 6–8 weeks' time, or when you've completed one of the programmes on pages 49–51. The Walking the Way to Health initiative found that simply getting people to monitor their steps over a 12-week period resulted in them increasing their walking by more than 1000 steps per day!

WARNING
If you ever feel chest pain or pressure, pain in the arms, neck or jaw, light-headedness or dizziness, palpitations, nausea, blurred vision or faintness, stop exercising and seek help if necessary.

Let's walk!

People often protest that they are too tired to exercise (see *No buts!*, pages 81–3) but the fact is, regular exercise improves sleep quality so that you wake up feeling more refreshed. One study of more than 700 people found that those who walked at least 1 km a day were a third less likely to have sleeping problems than those who didn't walk at all. Research from Seattle also found that the sleep quality of postmenopausal women improved when they got fitter.

Training know-how

We all know how to walk, but how do you turn it from a way of getting from A to B into a bona fide workout? The main reason why people don't achieve the benefits they expect from fitness walking is that they simply don't walk fast enough, for long enough or often enough. While any amount of walking – classified as a moderate exercise activity – will benefit your heart and general health, you need to approach walking much as you would any kind of exercise programme if you want genuine and lasting fitness benefits. That means you need a plan of progressive training, with specific goals and a set route to achieving them.

Planning your programme

How you play with variables such as distance, speed and frequency of walking – as well as terrain and incline – depends on what your goals are. So, as with any good fitness programme, we'll start by flexing a little mental muscle to help figure out what it is you want to achieve from your walking, and what your motivation is for embarking on a fitness programme; and then look at the principles of planning out what you need to do to get results.

You'll find some 8-week programmes on pages 41–51, designed to help you achieve specific health and fitness targets such as weight loss, greater mental well-being and improved muscle tone. But this section will show you how to tailor-make your own programme.

What do you want to gain – or lose?

Spend a few moments thinking about what has made you decide to get fit walking. This is about pinning down your motivation. You will find it really helpful later on – if you are beginning to lose interest or if other things are getting in the way of your programme – if you can pinpoint exactly what it was that made you start in the first place. (You can read more about motivation on page 79–81.)

Now think what you would like walking to have helped you achieve in, say, two months' time, or a year's time. This is the goal-setting part – and it is important that the goals you set are workable and sensible – and that they comply to the SMARTER goal-setting checklist, below.

> Everyone should take their dog for a walk every day. Even if they don't have one
>
> *Pers Astrand, Exercise Physiologist*

Smarter goal -setting

SMARTER stands for specific, measurable, achievable, relevant, time-related, exciting and recorded. If your goals don't quite match up, now is the time to adjust them, rather than plunging in head first and then finding that you are not achieving what you wanted, or that you have lost direction.

Here's an example of how a slight difference in the thought process and wording of a goal makes it SMART or stupid!

'I really must lose some weight and get fit before I go on holiday this summer.'

- Is the goal specific? No – we know that she wants to lose weight, but how much does she want to lose?
- Is it measurable? No – what does 'getting fit' actually mean to her? What criteria will she use to judge whether she has got fit?
- Is the goal achievable? It may be, but we don't know, as we don't know what she plans to do to lose weight and get fit, or when she is going on holiday! If it's in a fortnight and she plans to spend two hours each morning before work exercising, then certainly not.

- Is the goal relevant? In this context, relevant means 'does it mean something to you?' Goals that begin 'I must' or 'I should' often indicate that the person feels obliged to do something rather than being motivated by an innate desire to change or improve – so it may be that the pressure is coming from somewhere else.
- Is the goal time-related? Only partly. She says 'this summer', but it would be better if she were able to say 'in 10 weeks'.
- Is the goal exciting? Well, she certainly doesn't sound too enthused by it! Making goals that leave you cold rather than have you all fired up is making a rod for your own back. You'll be battling with motivation all the way.
- And finally, is the goal recorded? For what it's worth, yes! The goal is written down. It would be even better if she planned to gauge her progress by writing it all down in a training log.

This is how the goal might look if it were SMARTER.

'I am going to lose 7 lbs in the next eight weeks before I go on holiday, by walking briskly for an hour a day and improving my diet, so I feel great on the beach.'

More goal wisdom

Be positive and assertive with your wording! Not 'I'll try to… or 'I might…' but 'I will…' and 'I can…'. And try to make 'towards' goals rather than 'away from' ones. What does that mean? Well, it's the difference between saying, 'I want to adopt a healthier lifestyle, improve my fitness and have more energy,' and saying, 'I have got to stop living such an unhealthy lifestyle so I don't feel so tired all the time.'

Finally, write your goals down. It makes them feel more 'real' and it also gives you something to check back against. There may be times when you can't really fathom why you bothered starting an exercise regime, and re-reading why it was so important to you, and what you wanted to achieve, can really help you get back on track.

A word about motivation

There's nothing wrong with deciding to start exercising because you want to firm up your legs or lose your beer gut, but research shows that this kind of 'extrinsic' motivation, while good for getting you going, isn't as powerful as 'intrinsic' motivation in the long term. Intrinsic motivation is when you are driven by something deep within, such as wanting to feel better about yourself, to reduce your risk of disease or have more energy every day. It doesn't have a set endpoint.

OK, so now you have a clearer idea of what made you pick up this book, and about what you would like to achieve from walking. But how are you going to put it into practice? First off, let's have a look at the key factors that make a successful exercise regime.

Training principles

Make it challenging

Don't worry! This doesn't mean you have to feel as if you are knocking at death's door every time you work out – it simply means that if you don't make your body work harder than it is used to, then it will have no reason to get fitter. Whether you are a lifelong couch potato about to take your first foray into fitness or a highly active person, your fitness programme needs to be constantly adjusted to be more challenging if you are to continue making fitness gains. When you start, it may be that a 15-minute stride leaves you exhausted, but a few weeks down the line, once your body has made some of the adaptations described on page 7, that 15-minute route will no longer leave you sweat-soaked and breathless. Great. But that doesn't mean that you simply continue doing it, basking in the painlessness of it all! What it means is that you need to progress to something more challenging.

Sport scientists call this 'progressive overload'. That could be walking for longer, it could be walking the same route but faster, making some of your walks more intense (perhaps adding in some jogging intervals or hills), or it could mean simply doing the walk more frequently. The issue of frequency, intensity and time is often given the acronym FIT, and we'll look at the benefits and drawbacks of each of these variables in a moment.

Make it consistent

Whatever activity you do for fitness, do it consistently if you want results. It's only when the overload described above is repeated often enough that the body begins to make the adaptations. The stop-start cycle that many of us get stuck in with exercise and eating plans is not desirable – not only does it make the journey to fitness much more arduous, it also means that you are putting a lot of hard work in – albeit sporadically – without reaping the results. We'll talk a bit more about what constitutes consistency in *The fit bit*, on the next page. But rest assured, it doesn't mean you have to go training seven days a week.

Make time for rest

Yes, you need to increase the challenge of your workouts continually. And yes, you need to be consistent. But that doesn't mean that you should never have a day off! In fact, rest is a crucial part of training, as it is then that the body takes stock of the physical demands that have been placed upon it, and triggers the necessary adaptations, so that next time you make those demands, it will be more prepared to cope. There's no need to take a day's rest from your usual daily activities, however – it's only when you are working harder, by following a progressive walking programme, that you need to think about scheduling in rest days.

Keep it balanced

There's another term sport scientists like to bandy about – specificity. It means that to get good at what you want to do, you have to do it. So to become a proficient fitness walker, you need to go fitness walking. And while your heart doesn't know (or care!) whether you are walking, swimming or cycling, your nerves, muscles and the other connective tissues that are involved in walking will adapt more successfully to the task in hand if you walk, rather than do other activities. However, that doesn't mean that there is no place for alternative exercise in your fitness programme. Indeed, since walking is low impact and predominantly focused on the lower body, you may find it beneficial to also include some other types of activity to give a more rounded programme, minimise the risk of injury and earn a better body into the bargain. The workouts on pages 41–51 are designed to help you balance out and complement your programme.

The fit bit

So let's get back to the important issue of frequency, intensity and time. The way you manipulate these variables determines the results you are likely to get from your programme (I say likely, as every individual responds slightly differently, even to an identical exercise programme). It would be great if we could categorically say that by walking at 4 mph, for 30 minutes, 5 times a week, you would burn 1000 calories, but unfortunately it isn't that simple. But what does appear to be clear is that while any amount of walking at any pace is good, faster walking, and more of it, is better.

For example, research shows that women who usually walk at a brisk pace are about half as likely to develop heart disease than those who usually walk at a more leisurely pace and that increasing walking pace from three to four miles per hour can double fitness improvements.

Balancing time and intensity

The pace at which you walk is an individual thing – one person's sprint is another person's leisurely stroll. The goal is simply to increase your pace over a period of time. The important thing is to work at your own level. But that doesn't mean working at the same intensity every time; it means becoming adept at identifying your own perception of what is a 'comfortable' or a 'challenging' pace. You'll find that improving your technique (pages 27–30) will automatically accelerate you – and as you get fitter, you will hardly notice your speed creeping up.

That's not to say that walking at a slower pace has no benefits. For starters, at a leisurely pace you can probably walk for longer than you can if you go great guns, meaning that your calorie expenditure has the potential to be higher. See *Going steady vs flat out* opposite.

The good news about length and intensity is that as one goes up, the other goes down. In other words, you don't try to increase both

Going steady vs flat out

Walking at a **steady pace** for a prolonged period will yield myriad health and body benefits. The major boost is to the cardio-respiratory system (the heart and lungs), although moderate-paced walking will also teach your body to become more efficient at extracting oxygen from the blood and burning fat instead of carbohydrate as a fuel. Endurance in the lower body muscles will increase, and you will strengthen the connective tissues such as ligaments, tendons and cartilage. And, providing you do it for long enough, moderate-paced walking will burn a substantial amount of energy. A day's hike (6 hours cross-country walking, with a stop for lunch) for a 70 kg man will burn 2520 calories.

Faster walking, whether performed in one continuous effort or in 'intervals' (efforts separated by recovery periods), has some additional benefits. Working at a greater intensity of effort makes your heart more efficient at pumping blood around the body and gets you accustomed to working at a higher percentage of your maximum heart rate. It also raises what is called your lactate threshold – the point at which the working muscles produce more lactic acid (a by-product of metabolism), than can be cleared, so that it builds up in the muscle, hampering muscle contraction. Now, this is a good thing, as it means you can work at a higher percentage of your maximum without getting this lactic acid build-up. In other words, you can walk at the same speed with less effort, or walk even faster – increasing muscle strength and power and increasing energy expenditure still higher.

So which is best? The answer is that both steady-paced and faster walking have an important role to play in your overall fitness, which is why it is so essential to vary the speed and distance (or time) of your walks.

how *hard* you walk and how *long* you walk simultaneously. For best results, it's a good idea to work on increasing length in some sessions, and on increasing intensity in others.

Increasing time or distance – how to take your walking further

This is usually the preferred option for people who are new to exercise, as it doesn't take you beyond your 'comfort zone' in terms of how it will make you feel. The American Heart Association advises that exercise should boost heart rate to at least 55 per cent of its maximum, for at least 30 minutes five or more days a week – which is a pace that will not leave you beetroot-faced and breathless. This is the foundation on which we will build. You should be able to carry on a conversation and feel just slightly puffed and warm. Using the step count that you got from the 24-hour pedometer test in chapter 2, aim to increase the number of steps you take by 5–10 per cent per week, every week.

According to the journal *Sports Medicine*, once you have reached the magical 10,000-step mark, it's time to start thinking about injecting bouts of higher intensity exercise. Incidentally, while achieving 10,000 daily steps is a great achievement, it isn't carte blanche to sit back on your laurels! You need to be doing 12,500 to be considered 'highly active,' says the journal *Sports Medicine*.

Increasing intensity – how to rev up your walking workout

The obvious way to make your walking workout more intense is to walk faster (see page 30 for some tips and drills to help you do this). You can either do this continuously or in repeated bouts – you'll find both types of session in the walking programmes on pages 41–51. Another way of increasing the intensity, particularly if you don't feel able to walk any faster, is to hit the hills. Hills are a great way of getting more bang for your buck. Your heart rate will rise much more quickly and you'll gain strength in the lower body as well as aerobic fitness. You'll also hone in on your glute muscles, firming up your bottom on the way.

Going by instinct

Research from Duke University found that striking a balance between intensity and duration was what adults left to exercise without supervision would do. For eight months subjects exercised under supervision doing either low-intensity high-volume, high-intensity low volume or high-intensity high-volume workouts. At the end of the study, when asked to continue exercising without supervision, those who were doing low-intensity, long-duration preferred to do fewer minutes at a higher intensity, while those doing high-intensity, high-duration workouts tended to maintain the intensity but drop the duration. On average, left to their own devices, the participants did between 130–160 minutes per week (fitting in with the 30 minutes a day, most days of the week mantra) at a moderate intensity.

The question of frequency

How often do you need to walk? This is where we need to talk about the distinction between walking as part of your daily lifestyle activity and walking specifically for fitness. National guidelines recommend walking (or an equivalent moderate-intensity activity) for 30 minutes most days of the week to safeguard health. The American College of Sports Medicine (ACSM), a world authority on exercise, suggests that for fitness, we work at 55–90 per cent of our maximum heart rate for 20–60 minutes, 3–5 days per week. To ensure that you don't end up being one of the many people who say that 'walking doesn't work', I suggest that you see these 3–5 sessions as over and above your daily lifestyle walking rather than counting towards it.

Gauging effort levels

So how can you tell whether you are meeting the ACSM's recommended guidelines? How can you determine if you are working hard enough to achieve fitness benefits?

I think one of the easiest ways to gauge your effort level is to gauge how much conversation you could engage in while on the move. For example, could you chatter away endlessly – or would you find it difficult to eek out a 'good morning' as you stride past? The chart on page 42 outlines how to define four key effort levels for you to apply during your walking workouts.

Heart rate monitoring

Another, more scientific (but not necessarily superior) method of gauging intensity is to monitor your heart rate. As you learned in chapter 1, your heart rate rises in response to exercise – the harder you work, the higher it goes (although as you get fitter, you can do the same amount of work for less effort). So using your heart rate is a good way of checking that you are working at the right effort level. Everybody has a 'maximum' heart rate – the maximum number of times the heart can beat per minute – but actually measuring what that is involves a fairly strenuous maximal effort test. If you'd prefer to avoid that, then the usual way of estimating your maximum heart rate is simply to subtract your age from 220.

The 220 – age formula only gives a very broad approximation of heart rate, as real values can be as much as 20 beats out, but even if the actual value is a bit out, it still provides a useful gauge of your improvement, because when you get fitter, you will be able to work at a higher percentage of your estimated maximum without feeling so tired.

Once you've determined your age-predicted maximum, it's time for a little maths, as you use the information to determine what your own personal heart rate should be when working at different levels of intensity. Calculators at the ready?

The Karvonen Formula
First you need your resting heart rate value (see page 10).
Next, you need your age-predicted maximum heart rate.
Finally, you need to pick a percentage of your maximum at which you would like to work, to determine your heart rate at that intensity. Let's say in this example you want to know what your heart rate would be if you were working at 70 per cent of your maximum.

Percentage of max required % = (MHR – RHR) x percentage of max required % + RHR

Example: You are 35 years old. Your resting heart rate is 65 bpm. Age-determined MHR = 185.
70 per cent = (185 – 65) x 70% + RHR
70 per cent = 120 x 70% = 84 + 65
70 per cent = 149 bpm

So if our 35-year-old wanted to work at 70 per cent of his maximum heart rate, he would be aiming to get his heart rate up to 149 bpm. You can read about heart rate monitors in chapter 6.

How many calories am I burning?

A very broad guideline to the number of calories expended through walking is 100 calories per mile. Remember, though, that walking up hills and on uneven surfaces demands more calories, and that the heavier you are, the greater the energy demand for activity (so the higher the calorie expenditure). If you want a more accurate picture of the energy you burn through walking, use the following calculation:

Body weight in kg x average weekly distance walked in kms x 1.036

So, you know how often to walk, how hard to walk and for how long Let's now go on to look at how to maximise the benefits from your walking programme by addressing good technique and some essential before and after procedures.

Let's walk!

Walking may be the perfect activity to reduce anxiety, as studies have shown that moderate exercise is more effective than high-intensity exercise. One study found that a single walking session reduced tension as effectively as a tranquiliser, and the effects lasted longer.

3 Maximising the benefits

Walking is a fantastic form of exercise, and one of the most simple and natural forms of movement there is. But I'd argue that alone, it isn't sufficient to give you all-round fitness. For a start, it moves the body in just one plane of motion, forwards, and it relies almost entirely on the muscles of the lower body, and uses very little of the upper body musculature. I would say the same about any form of exercise done in isolation, so it's not a criticism of walking per se. This chapter is about maximising the benefits of fitness walking. Firstly, we will look at ideal technique and at how to increase your pace, then we'll look at how to warm up, cool down and stretch effectively and at some drills to enhance your walking technique.

Walk this way

You may be slightly incredulous that I am proposing to tell you how to do an activity you've been doing since you were a year old, but the fact is, there is an element of good technique in walking that will enable you to go faster and further and enhance your posture to boot.

Head: don't look down – look ahead (especially when going up hills). Also make sure that you don't crane your neck forward – a posture we often adopt when we are in a hurry.

Shoulders: keep them relaxed and allow the arms to move fluidly. Try shrugging them once before you start to ensure they aren't hunched and tense. Holding the shoulders and arms tense 'disconnects' the arms from the walking action, which is not what you want to do at all.

Arms: using your arms properly during walking increases energy expenditure by 5–10 per cent. If you are walking at a leisurely pace, the arms should be relaxed and slightly bent. As you speed up, the arms should be bent close to 90 degrees, and they should move forward and back in a straight plane, rather than crossing the body (known as 'chicken winging'). Your arms will help you go faster. Don't overdo the arm action though – there's no need for your hands to be swinging up level with your face! They should stop around sternum height. Hands should be relaxed but not floppy. Don't clench your fists.

Back: your back should be straight as you walk, allowing for its natural curves – so you shouldn't be leaning backwards or forwards. (A slight forward lean on hill climbs is acceptable.)

Abdominals: Keep your navel gently contracted to your spine – see *How to pull your tummy* in panel, opposite.

Pelvis and ribcage: keep some distance between the bottom of the ribcage and the top of the pelvis. Visualise leading from the sternum as you walk, to keep the chest open and the ribcage slightly forward. Imagine that your pelvis is a bucket of water, and you are aiming not to spill any by avoiding tipping it forward or back.

Legs: imagine your legs start at your waist, not your groin, and really extend them with each step.

Knees: the knee bends as the leg pulls through to strike the ground. Don't 'clench' your knees by tightening the thigh muscles – or lift the knees too high.

Ankles and feet: try to walk with 'loose' ankles. Imagine your foot is dangling rather than rigid between foot strikes. It is much easier to do this barefoot than in shoes or boots, but it is important as the ankle and knee joints work together rather than independently of one another – so rigid ankles have a detrimental effect on the knees too. As for the feet, the heel strikes the ground first, and then as the body moves forward you roll through to push off from the ball of the foot and toes.

How to pull your tummy in

If you think 'pull your tummy in' means suck in the stomach and hold your breath for as long as possible, think again! The first thing to do is learn how to identify and 'engage' the core muscles, which are the deep muscles of the back, waist and abdominals.

Identifying and engaging the core muscles is fundamental to good posture, core stability, a flatter abdomen and more efficient movement. To get a feel of the muscles you are trying to get to, which lie deep below the surface of the tummy, pretend to cough or sneeze, and you should feel the muscles contract involuntarily.

Now, while sitting on a chair, kneeling up on the floor, or on all fours, allow your tummy to relax completely. Start pulling up your pelvic floor (as if you were trying to stop yourself from peeing). Continue to pull in and up, using those muscles you located in the cough. Imagine you are doing up a zip from your pubic bone to your navel. The spine remains still as the core engages. You should be able to breathe freely throughout this movement, while sitting, standing or walking. If you find you have pushed your ribcage out and arched your back, try again. This time, draw the lower ribs down towards your pubic bone and think of pulling the navel back to the spine rather than puffing out the chest.

Taking it in your stride

Stride length is an individual thing – determined in part by your leg length, strength and flexibility (although leg length makes only about 3 per cent difference to the energy required to walk – so stubby legs are no excuse for reduced effort!). If you were to lean forward from standing, and catch yourself just as you were about to fall by extending one leg, the position of your feet should approximate your natural stride length.

The main drive for your stride comes from the leg when it is behind the body – it is the back leg that drives you forward, which is why your stride should be longer behind your body than it is in front. Thrusting out with your front leg, with the foot all tensed up, won't give you a more powerful stride. Getting the full power out of the push from the back leg as it rolls from heel to toe is the secret to powerful, efficient walking. Visualise the push starting way up at the top of the glutes.

Speeding up

As you get fitter, your pace will naturally quicken, but beware of the tendency to try to increase your speed by taking bigger strides. Actually, the more effective ploy is to take shorter but quicker steps. Race walkers train themselves to increase the number of steps they take per second, and to get full use out of the back part of the stride.

Loosen up!

Do not try to keep your torso still while your arms move back and forth. There is a natural spiralling action in which the rotation of the body around the spine is counterbalanced by the rotation of the hips. So, when the left knee goes forward (hips spiralling to the right) it is balanced by the right arm (torso spiralling to the left). This action is what connects the legs to the arms, and explains why the arms are so important in forward movement, be it walking or running.

Walk tall

Imagine you are growing taller with every step but not by straining and craning. Malcolm Balk, an Alexander Technique teacher and running coach, describes the feeling as 'falling upwards', which I think is spot-on.

Hitting the hills

Your heart rate will soon let you know that walking uphill is a whole different ball game from walking on the flat. You are lifting your body weight against gravity with every step, so the challenge is far greater. That can make for some excellent training, but it does help if you follow a few uphill technique pointers.

Don't try to take giant steps. It's more efficient to lean slightly into the slope and shorten your stride a little. Think of stairs – it is easier to power up closely-spaced steps than stride up huge, widely-spaced ones. Do make the most of the propulsive power of your arms. You'll find ascending a much easier prospect if you don't let your arms hang uselessly by your sides. Your heart rate will invariably go up, but think about maintaining

> Going to the gym didn't really work for me, so instead I have made a real effort to walk somewhere everyday. My fitness has really improved as a result.
>
> *Malcolm, from York*

an even effort rather than even pace. In other words, don't try to keep the same speedy pace that you had on the flat when you encounter a hill on your walk.

Warming up

Unlike running or a sport such as tennis or football, we walk every day, but that doesn't mean that you won't benefit from preparing for your workout by warming up. Bridging the gap between being still and moving not only helps your body avoid injury, it also enables you to get more out of your workout by priming the physiological and musculoskeletal systems.

One of the most important effects of a warm-up is that it raises body temperature. Chemical reactions involved in the production of energy happen more quickly in a warmer environment – for example, haemoglobin, the oxygen-carrying molecule, releases its oxygen more readily at higher temperatures.

Warming up also increases heart rate, and redirects blood flow away from the internal organs to the working muscles, bringing in oxygen and nutrients and removing metabolic waste products.

A warm-up mobilises and prepares the joints for walking. Articular cartilage, which is what cushions joint surfaces, does not have its own blood supply, but relies on nutrients being delivered by synovial fluid. Movement makes this fluid less 'sticky,' and squeezes it into the joint capsule, allowing it to soak the articular cartilage, and provide a protective cushion.

It also enhances neuromuscular pathways (the link between the muscular and nervous systems), thereby increasing the speed and efficiency of muscular contraction.

The walker's warm-up

So, how do you go about it? Warming up isn't rocket science, it simply means spending a few minutes doing gentle preparatory exercise to get you ready, physically and psychologically, for your workout. As a general rule, your warm-up should be at least five minutes long. If you are doing a short, fast workout, the warm-up should be longer and more thorough than if you are planning a slower, more prolonged walk. You should also spend longer warming up if it's freezing cold outside, or if you walk first thing in the morning, when body temperature is lower.

Although the primary muscles used in walking are all below the belt, a general mobilisation of all the body's major joints is still worthwhile. You don't want to be walking with tense shoulders or a stiff back. Mobilise the neck, shoulders, back, waist, hips, knees and ankles by following the sequence below. The idea is not to increase the range of motion but simply to work through it.

- Take your ear towards your shoulder, keeping the opposite shoulder relaxed. Move the head from side to side 8 times, and then look from side to side 8 times.
- Now bring your shoulders up towards your ears and roll them backwards and down again. Repeat 8 times.
- With your hands resting on your waist and your hips square, gently rotate the upper body from one side to the other, looking over your shoulder as you do so. Repeat 8 times.
- Now slide your hand down the outside of your thigh as you take the body to the side. Keep your hips in the centre. Alternate from side to side, 8 times.
- Draw a large imaginary circle with your hips: rest your hands on your hips and take your pelvis as far to the side, back and front as you can, keeping your legs straight but not locked. Do 4 circles in

one direction and 4 the other way.

- Pull one knee gently up to the chest, release and lift the other knee. Do 8 alternate lifts, and on the final lift on each side, circle the ankle 4 times in each direction.
- Now with both feet on the floor, tap each foot 16 times, as if you were tapping along to music.
- Finish by dropping your head to your chest and rolling down through your spine, with your knees slightly bent and tummy tight, until you reach the ground. Pause, then roll back up, 'rebuilding' the spinal column, vertebra by vertebra.

Nearly all sports advocate walking as part of a warm-up – so once you have mobilised, simply begin walking at a slow pace. Add in some bouts of walking on your heels and then on your toes and gradually pick up speed to your desired pace for the session.

TIP

If you have been sitting down all day – or even standing – having a brief lie-down on the floor before you start your warm-up will help to decompress your spine and prevent you taking the day's tensions on your walk. Lie on your back with your knees bent and feet flat on the floor, arms resting by your sides with palms facing upwards.

Cool-down and stretching

Once your walking workout is over, come to a gradual halt, rather than stopping suddenly. This is particularly important if you have been working hard, as blood will be pumping around the body very fast, and stopping suddenly can cause it to pool in the veins and make you feel dizzy or nauseous. A cool-down period also helps dispel the waste products that have accumulated in the muscles.

When you have spent a couple of minutes slowing down, you could repeat some of the mobilisations you did in the warm-up, but if you are short on time, move straight on to a thorough stretch.

The case for stretching

When we move, muscles naturally shorten and contract. Without flexibility work, this can cause an 'adaptive shortening' of the muscle and connective tissue, leaving our bodies feeling stiffer and reducing our range of movement. After a period of prolonged muscle contraction (such as a workout), muscles can take up to two hours to be restored to their resting length – but just a few minutes' stretching will enable this to happen much more quickly. Stretching also speeds up the removal of waste products and the arrival of fresh nutrients to the recovering muscle.

It's not just exercise that causes muscles to get shorter and tighter, either. For those of us who spend many hours each day sitting, the muscles that bear the brunt of this position – and those that are constantly relaxed due to it – become imbalanced. In time, shortened muscles eventually force the body out of alignment and, assisted by gravity, create poor posture.

So, I think you'll agree, investing a little time after your walks to mitigate the shortening and imbalancing effects of exercise is worthwhile. With a little perseverance and regular practice, stretching can maintain good range of motion and increase the length of the muscles or, at least, help prevent them from shortening – which will give you a longer, sleeker look, better posture, a more supple body and put a spring in your step.

Why stretch?

- Recovery time between workouts is shortened
- Injuries may be more easily prevented
- Muscle fibres are restored to their optimal length
- Posture and flexibility are improved
- Workouts are more efficient
- Circulation is increased – allowing your body to flush out waste products and recover more easily
- Helps mental relaxation and focus.

Getting it right

If you are going to spend precious minutes stretching out, make sure you do it properly, to gain maximum benefits. Bear the following points in mind.

- Are you doing the stretch properly? Just a tiny error in body positioning can greatly reduce the effectiveness of a stretch, so follow instructions carefully, or ask a trainer to demonstrate what to do. You should stretch to the point at which you feel tension and a slight pulling sensation in the muscle but not pain. Hold this position until the 'stress-relaxation' response occurs and the force on the muscle decreases. Then increase the stretch if you can, and continue to hold.

- Are you holding it for long enough? You need to go for 30 seconds to improve flexibility and ideally repeat each stretch twice. A study published in the journal *Physical Therapy* found that people who stretched each muscle group for 30 seconds a day made greater increases in their range of motion than those who stretched each muscle for 15 seconds, but that no further benefits were seen in stretching for 60 seconds.

- Are you stretching the muscles you need to? For example, the shins and hips often get neglected while we all remember to stretch calves, hamstrings and quads.

- Are you doing it regularly enough? The American College of Sports Medicine recommends a minimum of 2–3 times per week. Try to stretch after every workout when your muscles are nicely warm, to keep your joints and muscles healthy and mobile.

The walker's stretch

Hamstrings

Stand facing a support between knee and hip height. Extend one leg and place it on the support, with the foot relaxed. Your supporting leg should be perpendicular to the floor. Now hinge forward from the hips (don't round the back), keeping the pelvis level and the knee of the extended leg straight. Feel the stretch along the back of the supported thigh. To emphasise the outer hamstring, bring the leg slightly across the midline of your body and rotate the hip joint slightly inwards. To emphasise the

hamstrings closest to the middle of the body, turn out at the hip joint and take the leg slightly away from the midline of the body. (You don't need to pull your toes back towards you – the only reason this intensifies the stretch is because it adds the sciatic nerve into the equation.)

Upper and lower calves and feet

Stand facing a support, feet a stride length apart, with back leg straight and front leg bent. Press the back heel into the floor so that you experience a stretch in the middle of the calf muscle. Turn toes slightly inwards to focus on the outer side of the calf. Hold.

Now bring the back leg in a little, bend the knee and flex the hips, so that the stretch moves down to the lower part of the calf and Achilles tendon.

Finally, with both legs still bent, place the toes of the back foot up against the heel of the front foot to stretch the muscles of the foot.

Quads

Stand tall with feet parallel and then lift your right heel, taking your right hand behind you to grab the foot. Bring your pelvis in to a neutral position and gently press your foot into your hand, keeping your knees close together. It doesn't matter if your stretching thigh is in front of the supporting one, as long as you feel a stretch.

Hip and iliotibial band

Stand tall, and cross one leg behind the other, sliding it away from you until you feel a stretch in the back leg hip. Bend the supporting leg and lean your torso in the direction the back leg is stretching.

Hip flexors

Assume a lunge position, allowing your back knee to go to the floor, and your toes to face down. Tighten your tummy muscles and extend forwards from your back hip, until your front knee is at 90 degrees. You should feel a stretch along the front of your hip joint and thigh.

Shins

Kneel on a mat with a rolled up towel under your feet. Gently lower your weight onto your haunches and feel a stretch along the front of your shins and ankles. To increase the stretch, place both hands on the floor, and lift each leg alternately.

Adductors

Sit on the floor with your knees drawn into your chest and feet flat on the floor. Drop your knees open to the sides and use your elbows to gently press the legs open. Don't round the back, sit up tall. Hold, then extend the legs out to the sides and hinge forward from the hips.

Glutes/abductors

Sit against a wall with your legs out-stretched. Cross your left foot over your right thigh and put your foot flat on the floor. Now take your right arm around your left knee and gently pull it around towards your shoulder (rather than hugging directly to your chest), sitting up tall.

Hip rotators

Lie face up on the floor and bring one knee into your chest, the other leg flat on the floor. Now grasp the ankle of the bent leg and, stabilising the knee with your other hand, gently pull it across your body until you feel a deep hip stretch in the lifted leg.

Lower back

Roll onto your back, bend your knees in towards your chest and link your arms around them. Pull your knees towards your shoulders, pressing your lower back into the floor. Then take your arms to a crucifix position, and alternately drop your knees down to each side.

4 The walking workouts

The workouts in this section are designed to get you going on your walking programme, whether you want to walk for health, weight loss or improved fitness. There is nothing mystical or magical about these walking programmes – they include the elements of progression explained on pages 8–13 and include a variety of different types of workout to add interest and challenge. If you prefer to design your own regime, that's absolutely fine, or you may wish to take elements from those shown below and adapt them to suit your own goals.

The effort chart *Can we talk?* describes the intensity of effort you should feel when working at the levels given in each programme. When you get to the end of an 8-week programme, remember to keep increasing the challenge – either by increasing the intensity or number of the intervals or hills, or the length or intensity of the sessions. Or try adding the *Outdoor circuit* from the *Fighting fit* workout. The two workouts at the end of the section are designed to 'balance' your walking programme: the first by strengthening the muscles needed to maximise your walking capacity; the second by working muscles that don't get much of a look in during walking.

Can we talk?

Level 1	'I could walk and talk all day' pace	Use this pace for your warm-up, for longer steady walks, or when you are first starting out on regular training. This is also the pace to go for during the 'recovery' sections of your interval training. Equates to 55–70 per cent max heart rate
Level 2	'Comfortable conversation' pace	Use this pace on your steady walks. Equates to 70–75 per cent max heart rate
Level 3	'I'd like to say a few words' pace – can say the odd sentence and reply	Aim for this pace on 'threshold' walks, hill climbs and intervals. Equates to 75–80 per cent max heart rate
Level 4	'Don't speak to me' pace	Use this pace on more intense hill work and shorter intervals. Equates to 80–90 per cent max heart rate

In the workouts L1, L2, L3 and L4 relate to the intensities described.

The well-being workout (page 49)

This programme is all about enhancing your physical and mental well-being and getting you accustomed to becoming more active. It's a great place to start for anyone who is time-crunched, stressed, or simply out of the activity habit for any reason. The goal is to gradually increase your daily activity to show how achievable it is – and what the benefits are. See *Helping your heart* to find out how regular walking is protecting your cardiovascular system from disease, or *Brain booster* to read about the mental benefits.

You will notice that on some walks I have highlighted a type of 'focus' – internal or external. With the internal focus walks, the idea is to get back in touch with your body – we often lose touch with ourselves when we are stressed, depressed, after illness or a long period of inactivity. Focus on your breathing and posture on these walks – picture your heart pumping blood around your body, your lungs expanding to suck in oxygen and feel tension melt away. Pick somewhere where it is safe to walk without paying full attention to what's going on around you – for example, not where you will have to cross lots of roads. You may find it helps to create a 'mantra'– a short, simple phrase that you repeat in your head to stay focused (eg. *I am calm and I am strong*).

Brain booster

Walking is a rhythmical, simple form of prolonged exercise – the perfect type of movement to assist in creative thinking and problem solving, research shows. The increased blood flow to the brain resulting from aerobic exercise also helps to optimise mental functions such as memory, reaction time and concentration. Research from Washington University found that a brisk 10-minute walk left subjects feeling more relaxed and energetic.

The reason most frequently given to explain why exercise makes us feel good is the flood of endorphins it causes (the body's own morphine-like happy hormones), but increasingly research is questioning the role of endorphins and pointing more towards a psychological rather than physiological cause.

Exercise provides a distraction from the grind of daily life – giving us 'time out' from the rat race. It also gives a sense of accomplishment (particularly when it's over and you are in the shower!) which sport psychologists call 'mastery', boosting self-esteem and proffering a sense of control over our lives.

Another way exercise can be positively beneficial is by enhancing body image – not just by improving the physical body itself, but by improving our attitudes towards our bodies. How? Well, as you become regularly active and fit, you begin to appreciate the wondrous piece of machinery that you own and see yourself in a broader context that simply judging yourself on what youlook like or how much you weigh.

On the external focus walks, the idea is to turn your eyes outwards and take in what's going on around you. Many of us spend our days focusing our eyes no further than a couple of feet away to the computer screen, so let your focus widen and your brain be distracted from daily worries and pressures. Use all your senses – visual, auditory, kinaesthetic, taste and smell – to help you immerse yourself in the world around you. It helps to be somewhere interesting when you do these walks – a treadmill would not be ideal – but a nature trail, a towpath or even a buzzing urban street would give you plenty of stimuli. Don't try to problem-solve – walk in the present. If no focus is mentioned, do what feels right at the time.

The weight-loss workout (page 50)

A study from Duke University Medical Centre suggests that not only can 30 minutes of daily walking prevent weight gain in most sedentary people, but that additional exercise time can aid fat loss. They also found that while the amount of exercise determined total body weight change and fat loss, exercise intensity seemed to be the primary determinant of gain in lean body mass (muscle).

The American College of Sports Medicine's position stand on exercise and weight loss recommends building up to 200–300 minutes of activity per week. Sounds daunting, huh? But there are two points to bear in mind. First, those two words 'building up' – you don't have to do it from day one! Second, that 200–300 minutes breaks down to 40–60 minutes, 5 days a week – and it can incorporate both bona fide 'workouts' and your daily lifestyle activity. I've included a list of activities on pages 46–7 you can think about doing alongside your walking to maximise energy expenditure, but remember, you also need to be vigilant about how much energy you are taking in, if you are to meet your weight-loss goals. I've also included 10-minute booster walks, which you don't need to get changed for – simply slip on your walking shoes and walk for 10 minutes, around the shopping centre, the

Helping your heart

Becoming aerobically fit enables the heart to achieve the same amount of 'work' for less effort. It can pump out more blood with each beat (stroke volume) and can therefore supply the working muscles with oxygenated blood without having to increase the number of times it beats by as much. Long-term regular aerobic exercise also increases the amount of blood by 10–15 per cent, further reducing demand on the heart.

The Nurse's Health Study found that walking briskly for at least one hour a week offered moderate protection against stroke, too. Women who walked at the quickest paces had the greatest reduction in risk.

Regular aerobic exercise has positive effects on four of the main cardiovascular disease risk factors: blood pressure (people with hypertension are three times more likely to experience heart disease), cholesterol profile (exercise lowers total cholesterol and increases the amount of HDL cholesterol), the risk of diabetes and excess body weight.

car park, the block – wherever you are! It is 5 minutes out and 5 minutes back.

- Don't refuel with calorific energy bars and sports drinks.
- Don't try to starve yourself – you won't have enough energy for sustained walking.
- Drink plenty of water – your body may mistake dehydration for hunger.
- Consider doing the *Body-balancing workout*, or a gym strength programme, to increase muscle tone and maximise daily energy expenditure.
- Do be careful that you don't inadvertently reward yourself for your walking with more time sprawled on the sofa – be as active as you can.

Measurements

The scales don't tell the full story with weight loss, since muscle weighs more than body fat due to its high water content. Measuring four key body sites is a good way of keeping tabs on your progress.

Waist – measure around the narrowest part of your midriff.
Navel – measure around the midriff directly over the bellybutton.
Hips – measure across the top of the buttock cheeks.
Thighs – stand with feet together, measure eight inches up from the top of your kneecap and take a circumference measurement of your thighs.

Let's walk

The incidence of type 2 (adult onset) diabetes has shown an alarming increase in recent years. Regularly active adults have a 42 per cent lower risk of getting the disease, as a higher fitness level has been shown to increase insulin sensitivity and enhance glucose transportation. And to prove that you don't need to be running marathons to benefit, the Nurses' Health Study found that women who walked briskly for three hours a week reduced their risk of diabetes as much as women who exercised vigorously for an hour and a half a week. The more time women spent walking and the faster they walked, the less likely they were to develop the disease.

Other daily activities to maximise calorie expenditure

- Going up and down the stairs burns nearly 100 calories in 10 minutes for a 10-stone woman. Leave stuff at the bottom of the stairs and take things up one by one, rather than piling it up and taking it all at once to guarantee you'll get your 10 minutes in each day.
- Park further from the supermarket entrance so you have further to carry bags or push the trolley.
- Stand up when you are on the phone and move around.

- Walk to a sandwich shop further away at lunchtime.
- Leave the car at home for shorter journeys.
- Meet a friend for a walk and talk, rather than sitting for coffee.
- Don't email or call colleagues in the same building – go and talk to them.
- Get up during every advertisement break and walk around – and hide the remote control. Every time you switch channels from the sofa, you conserve 10 calories. It might not sound much, but it adds up to an additional pound of fat gained per year.
- Get active between the sheets! Even kissing burns 60 calories an hour, but throw in a pillow fight, a sensual massage and a passionate sex session and you'll easily rival a workout!
- Don't stand still throwing the ball for your dog – run after it yourself, too.
- Never stand still on the escalators and eschew lifts.
- Have a spring clean! A combination of dusting, mopping, scrubbing and sweeping will melt off 400 calories in an hour and your house will be gleaming. Or redecorate! There's nothing like a fresh coat of paint to give a room a new lease of life. You'll have to move the furniture first, of course, and you'll burn over 300 calories per hour of painting.

The fighting fit workout (page 51)

Think walking is for wimps? This workout will convince you otherwise! The hill sessions and interval workouts will have your heart rate soaring, get your muscles firm and strong and prime your cardiovascular system. You can walk-run (see below) or simply change pace during the intervals, and remember your climbing technique for the hill sessions (pages 30–31). On the 'threshold' walks, think about being at a 'comfortably uncomfortable' pace – the highest pace you can sustain for the time given. The exercises in the *Outdoor circuit* are briefly described below.

Run-walking

Run-walking is a strategy that many runners use, not just as beginners but as a way of being able to maintain fitness without putting undue stress on the body. It's a fantastic introduction to running, and even if you don't have any intention of becoming a runner it will multiply the benefits you get from your workouts by increasing their intensity, boosting bone density and maximising calorie expenditure. To start with, aim to walk for double the length of time that you run (for example, if you walk for 2 minutes, you'd run for 1 minute) and keep the intervals short so that you don't run out of puff before you've barely got going. Once that is comfortable, go for a 1:1 ratio (equal minutes' walking and running) and then aim to run for double the amount of time that you walk. From there, you can either extend the length of the intervals or cut out the walking altogether and give prolonged running a try. There's no harm in mixing walking and running workouts up during your training week for variety and balance.

Day/week	Mon	Tue	Wed	Thur	Fri	Sat	Sun
1	Walk 20 mins at L1 External focus	Walk 10 mins at L2 Internal focus plus *Walk away from injury workout*	Walk 20 mins at L1 External focus	Walk 10 mins at L2 Internal focus plus *Walk away from injury workout*	Walk 20 mins at L1 with 5 x 1 mins at L3 included	REST	Walk 45 mins at L1
2	Walk 25 mins at L1 External focus	Walk 10 mins at L2 Internal focus plus *Walk away from injury workout*	Walk 25 mins at L1 External focus	Walk 10 mins at L2 Internal focus plus *Walk away from injury workout*	Walk 20 mins at L1 with 6 x 1 mins at L3 included	REST	Walk 45 mins at L1
3	Walk 20 mins at L2 External focus	Walk 15 mins at L2 Internal focus plus *Walk away from injury workout*	Walk 20 mins at L2 External focus	Walk 15 mins at L2 Internal focus plus walk away from injury workout	Walk 20 mins at L1 with 7 x 1 mins at L3 included	REST	Walk 50 mins at L1
4	Walk 20 mins at L2 External focus	Walk 10 mins at L3 Internal focus plus *Walk away from injury workout*	Walk 20 mins at L2 External focus	Walk 10 mins at L3 Internal focus plus walk away from injury workout	Walk 20 mins at L1 with 8 x 1 mins at L3 included	REST	Country hike/park wander varied effort L1–4 1hr
5	Walk 25 mins at L2 External focus	Walk 15 mins at L3 Internal focus plus *Body-balancing workout*	Walk 25 mins at L2 External focus	Walk 15 mins at L3 Internal focus plus body balancing workout	Walk 20 mins at L1 with 5 x 30 secs at L4 included	REST	Walk 50 mins at L2
6	REST	Walk 20 mins at L2 with 6 x 30 secs at L4 included	Walk 30 mins at L2 External focus plus *Body-balancing workout*	Walk 20 mins at L3 Internal focus	Walk 20 mins at L2 with 5 x 30 secs at L4 included	*Body-balancing workout*	Walk 55 mins at L1
7	REST	Walk 25 mins at L2 with 8 x 30 secs at L4 included	Walk 30 mins at L2 External focus plus *Body-balancing workout*	Walk 20 mins at L3 Internal focus	Walk 20 mins at L2 with 5 x 30 second hill climbs at L4 included	*Body-balancing workout*	Walk 1 hr at L2
8	REST	Walk 25 mins at L2 with 8 x 30 secs at L4 included	Walk 30 mins at L2 External focus plus *Body-balancing workout*	Walk 20 mins at L3 Internal focus	Walk 20 mins at L2 with 5 x 30 second hill climbs at L4 included	*Body-balancing workout*	Country hike 1.5 hours varying effort L1–4

The weight-loss workout

Day/week	Mon	Tue	Wed	Thur	Fri	Sat	Sun
1	Walk 20 mins at L1 plus 10-minute booster	10-min booster and *Walk away from injury workout*	Walk 25 mins at L1 plus 10-min booster	*Walk away from injury workout and 10-min booster*	Walk 20 mins at L2	REST	Walk 45 mins at L1
2	Walk 25 mins at L1 plus 1 10-minute booster	10-min booster and *Walk away from injury workout*	Walk 25 mins at L1 plus 10-min booster	*Walk away from injury workout and 10-min booster*	Walk 25 mins at L2	REST	Walk 50 mins at L1
3	Walk 30 mins at L1 plus 10-minute booster	10-min booster and *Walk away from injury workout*	Walk 25 mins at L2 plus 10-min booster	*Walk away from injury workout and 10-min booster*	Walk 30 mins at L2 with 5 x 1 min at L3	REST	Walk 55 mins at L1
4	Walk 20 mins at L2 plus 10-min booster	10-min booster and *Body-balancing workout*	Walk 25 mins at L2 plus 10-min booster	*Body-balancing workout and 10-min booster*	Walk 30 mins at L2 with 6 x 1 min at L3	10-min booster	Country hike varied effort at L1–4
5	Walk 25 mins at L2 plus 10-min booster	10-min booster and *Body-balancing workout*	Walk 30 mins at L2 plus 10-min booster	*Body-balancing workout and 10-min booster*	Walk 30 mins at L2 with 8 x 1 min at L3	REST	Walk 1 hr at L2
6	Walk 30 mins at L2 plus 10-min booster	10-min booster and *Body-balancing workout*	Walk 30 mins at L2 incorporating 5 x 30 sec hill climbs at L4 plus 10-min booster	*Body-balancing workout and 10-min booster*	Walk 30 mins at L2 with 10 x 1 min at L3	REST	Walk 1 hr at L2
7	Walk 20 mins at L3 plus 10-min booster	10-min booster and *Body-balancing workout*	Walk 30 mins at L2 incorporating 6 x 30 sec hill climbs at L4 plus 10-min booster	*Body-balancing workout and 10-min booster*	Walk 30 mins at L2 with 6 x 30 secs at L4	REST	Walk 1 hr hilly route at L2 with L4 on inclines
8	Walk 20 mins at L3 plus 10-min booster	2 x 10-min booster and *Body-balancing workout*	Walk 35 mins at L2 incorporating 8 x 30 sec hill climbs at L4 plus 10-min booster	*Body-balancing workout and 2 x 10-min boosters*	Walk 30 mins at L2 with 8 x 30 secs at L4	10-min booster	Walk 1 hr hilly route at L2 with L4 on inclines

Day/week	Mon	Tue	Wed	Thur	Fri	Sat	Sun
1	Interval session 30 mins: alternating 2 mins at L2 and 1 min at L3	Steady walk: 45 mins L2	*Body-balancing workout*	Interval session 30 mins: alternating 2 mins at L2 and 1 min at L3	Steady walk: 45 mins L2	REST	45-min walk at L3 including *Outdoor circuit*
2	Interval session 30 mins: alternating 1 min at L2 and 1 min at L3	Steady walk: 45 mins L2	*Body-balancing workout*	Interval session 30 mins: alternating 1 min at L2 and 1 min at L3	Steady walk: 45 mins (with 10 mins at L3 in the middle)	REST	50-min walk at L3 including *Outdoor circuit*
3	Interval session 30 mins: alternating 1 min at L2 and 1 min at L4	Steady walk: 50 mins L2	*Body-balancing workout*	Interval session 30 mins: alternating 1 min at L2 and 1 min at L4	Steady walk: 45 mins (with 10 mins at L3 in the middle)	REST	55-min walk at L3 including *Outdoor circuit*
4	Interval session 30 mins: alternating 1 min at L2 and 2 mins at L3	Steady walk: 50 mins at L2 with 2 x 10 mins at L3 incorporated	*Body-balancing workout*	Interval session 30 mins: alternating 1 min at L2 and 2 mins at L3	REST	Threshold session 20 mins at L3	Day hike
5	Interval session 36 mins: alternating 1 min at L2 and 2 mins at L3	Steady walk: 50 mins at L2 with 2 x 10 mins at L3 incorporated	*Body-balancing workout*	Interval session 36 mins: alternating 1 min at L2 and 2 mins at L3	REST	Threshold session 20 mins at L3	60-min walk at L2 including 10 x 25 m hill climbs at L4
6	Interval session 36 mins: alternating 1 min at L2 and 2 mins at L4	Steady walk: 50 mins at L2 with 3 x 8 mins at L3 incorporated	*Body-balancing workout*	Interval session 36 mins: alternating 1 min at L2 and 2 mins at L4	REST	Threshold session 25 mins at L3	60-min walk at L2 including 12 x 25 m hill climbs at L4
7	Interval session 40 mins: alternating 1 min at L2 and 3 mins at L3	Steady walk: 1 hr with 3 x 10 mins at L3 incorporated	*Body-balancing workout*	Interval session 40 mins: alternating 1 min at L2 and 3 mins at L3	REST	Threshold session 25 mins at L3	Day hike
8	Interval session 40 mins: alternating 2 mins at L3 and 1 min at L4	Steady walk: 1 hr with 3 x 10 mins at L3 incorporated	*Body-balancing workout*	Interval session 40 mins: alternating 1 min at L3 and 3 mins at L4	REST	Threshold session 30 mins at L3	60-min walk at L3 including *Outdoor circuit*

Outdoor circuit exercises

Each of the outdoor circuit 'stations' is performed when you reach the appropriate piece of equipment, so you can do the exercises in any order, before continuing with your walk.

Park bench station

Firm up your upper arms by sitting on a bench, gripping the edge, with your legs straight out in front of you and your bottom just off the front of the bench. Lower yourself by bending your arms until your forearms reach a right angle. Straighten and repeat. Then, go to the back of the bench and do a set of modified push-ups, with your hands shoulder-width apart (not shown). Do 10 repetitions of each and repeat.

Step shuttle

Find a flight of steps, and sprint up as fast as you can for 15 seconds. Then turn around and come back down, leaping laterally from foot to foot. Repeat twice more. This works on leg strength and tones the bum. Use your arms to propel you, and keep your torso upright.

Kerb lunge

Stand facing a kerb, a large stride away from the raise. Take a big step forward, front foot landing on the raise, bending both knees and allowing the back knee to almost touch the ground. Pause, then push through the front heel to raise yourself back up. Immediately step forward with the other leg. Continue until you have done 20 repetitions. This is a great firmer for the back and front of the thighs and bottom.

Kerb or low wall balance

Use the edge of a kerb or a low wall to walk along as if it were a balance beam. Walk tall, and try to place your foot directly in front of your back foot, squeezing your inner thighs. This also hones your balance and co-ordination. Take 20 steps, changing direction if necessary.

Railing pull-up

Hook a sweatshirt or tracksuit top through a set of railings and take an arm in each hand. Lean back slowly until your arms are extended, then pull yourself back towards the rails. This will strengthen the upper and middle back and biceps. If you can find a cycle rack, you can dispense with the sweatshirt and do it by holding the top railing and shifting your body underneath (use an underhand grip). Do 10 repetitions.

The walk away from injury workout

This workout will help you build the strength, balance and flexibility needed to become a proficient, injury-free walker. Try to do it 2–3 times a week – it should take about 20 minutes and all you need is a mat or towel, a cushion, a step or stair and a resistance tube (you could even use a bicycle inner tube or an old pair of tights!).

Ankle pull

Why? To strengthen the tibialis anterior muscle in the shin and actively stretch the calves, reducing the likelihood of shin splints (see page 97).

Hook a resistance tube or band around your instep, with the ends attached to something solid and some tension in the band. Now, resisting the pull of the band against your foot, bring the toes up towards the shins. Pause, lower and repeat. Swap feet. Do 2 sets of 8 repetitions.

Balancing act

Why? To strengthen the muscles around the ankle, avoid inflammation of the ankle ligaments and improve balance.

Stand on one bare foot for 30 seconds while kicking the other leg back and forward. Progress to doing this on an unstable surface, such as a cushion or mattress, rebounder or a designated 'wobble' board. Swap sides. **1 on each side**

Bridge

Why? To strengthen the gluteals, lower back and inner thighs and improve pelvic stability.

Lie on the floor with your knees bent, feet flat and a cushion between your knees. Place your arms flat on the floor behind you. Raise your body up enough to allow your pelvis to clear the floor, hold for 5 seconds, then release without dropping the cushion. Once you can do this comfortably, progress to a walking bridge, in which you walk one leg a couple of inches away from the pelvis, then the other, then bring them back alternately. Do 2 sets of 8 repetitions.

Toe curler

Why? To improve lower leg muscle balance and strengthen the calf muscles.

Stand on a stair barefoot, with your toes extending over the edge. Bend your toes as if gripping the edge for a count of two, then flex them upwards and hold for two. Then turn around and, with your heels dropping over the edge of the step, raise up on to your toes and then drop slowly back down, keeping the gluteals contracted. **2 x 8 of each**

Abdominal hollow and pelvic tilt

Why? This strengthens the deep abdominal muscles which contribute to good posture.

Lie face down with your hands under your forehead and your head in line with your body. Keeping the rest of your body relaxed, tilt your pelvis by curling your pubic bone up towards your navel (effectively flattening the curve of the lower back). Now inhale and peel your navel off the floor towards your spine, trying to lift your abdominals off the floor. Hold for 6 seconds, breathing freely, then relax. Do not lift your hipbones off the floor or contract your back. **1 x 8**

Single leg squat

Why? To strengthen the muscles supporting the knee joint to promote good alignment. To improve hip and knee stability and work the innermost quadriceps (the vastus medialis obliquus), by locking the knee out to full extension.

Stand with your feet 8 inches apart and your arms out to the side for balance. Lift your left leg off the floor, and slowly bend your right leg, keeping your knee over your fourth toe and not allowing your pelvis to tip to the side. Straighten and repeat. Swap sides. **2 x 8**

Prone bent leg lift

Why? To strengthen the gluteus muscles without aid from the hamstrings – to improve pelvic stability – and actively stretch the hip flexors.

Lie face down on a mat (head resting on the backs of your

hands) and lift your bent right leg up so that your lower leg is at a right angle to the floor. Squeeze your glutes together and, pressing your hipbones into the floor, raise your leg a few inches off the floor. Hold for 10 seconds then lower and repeat. Swap sides. **2 x 8**

The body-balancing workout for walkers

This circuit-style workout is designed to tone and strengthen the muscle groups that don't get much of a workout from walking. I have interspersed the exercises with high impact moves to boost bone density and maximise calorie expenditure. The 20-minute workout should be done 2–3 times per week for results and you will need a resistance tube (or hand weights), a step or stair and either a real or imaginary skipping rope or a rebounder. Warm up first and wear supportive shoes. As you get fitter, increase the resistance on the strength exercises and increase the aerobic intervals in 30-second stages. (Any of the aerobic intervals can be swapped for each other.) Cool down and stretch afterwards.

Incline push-up
Works: chest, shoulders, triceps, abdominals.

Find a sturdy support between chest and knee height (the lower, the harder). Form a straight line from your head to your toes, with your arms straight and shoulder-width apart or a little wider, your

abdominals contracted and your head in line with your spine. Lower the body towards the support by bending your arms. When your arms reach a right angle, pause, and straighten to repeat. (Full push-ups are fine if you can maintain a straight body position.)

Aerobic interval: skipping

Boosts bone density and improves cardiovascular fitness.

With a real or imaginary skipping rope, skip for 1 minute, keeping your feet low and ensuring your heels touch down. If you prefer, you can do your imaginary skipping on a rebounder.

Single arm row

Works: upper and middle back, biceps, back of shoulder.

Stand side on to your support, with your back straight and one knee and hand resting on the support. Keep your abdominals contracted. Take a weight or the end of an anchored resistance tube in your free hand, and allow it to dangle below your shoulder. Now, bring the weight up towards your shoulder by bending at the elbow, but without twisting the torso or using momentum. Pause, then lower.

Aerobic interval: explosive step-ups

Boosts bone density and improves cardiovascular fitness. Stand in front of a step or the lowest stair and spring up with one foot and then the other for 1 minute. (One foot is always on the ground level.)

Leg crossover

Works inner thighs. Hook one end of a resistance band around something sturdy and loop the other end around your right leg. Shuffle away from the attachment point until there is enough tension in the band, and your right leg is lifted out to the side. Now bring your right leg in towards the centre, taking it just across the left leg, toes facing directly forward. Do not allow the hip of the supporting leg to 'dip,' and keep the core engaged. Release the leg back to the start position and repeat.

Aerobic interval: hopping

Improves balance and bone density.

Place a sheet of A4 paper on the floor (not a slippery magazine) and attempt to hop on it with your right foot for 30 seconds. Swap sides for a further 30 seconds.

Shoulder press

Works: deltoids and triceps and upper back.

Sit on an upright bench or chair with back straight and a weight in each hand, resting on the shoulders with palms facing each other. Extend the arms over the head, allowing them to rotate so that when the arms are straight, the palms are facing the front. You should be able to see your arms in your peripheral vision as they are raised – don't take the arms behind the line of the head. You can also do this exercise with a resistance tube threaded underneath the bench or chair.

Aerobic interval: power squat

Works: all the lower body muscles, including front and back of thighs and bottom, and boosts bone density.

Stand with your feet 6–8 in apart, arms across your chest and hands on opposite shoulders. Take your weight back into your heels and lower your body by bending your legs, leading with your bottom, and with knees directly over the middle toes. From the squat position, leap as high as you can in the air, landing directly back into the squat and take off again immediately. Aim for 10–15 jumps.

Hip abduction

Works: outer thighs, hips.

Lie on your side with your legs 'stacked' from ankle to hip (directly on top of one another) and your weight supported on your elbow – don't let your body sink into the supporting arm. Raise your top leg a few inches from the supporting one, keeping the toes facing directly forwards and ensuring that the leg lengthens out of the hip socket as

you extend it. Lower, repeat all repetitions and swap sides. To progress: Tie a resistance tube around both ankles to create extra resistance other than gravity to overcome as you lift your leg, or use an ankle weight.

Toe touchdowns
Works: all abdominals.

Lie on your back with your knees bent and feet flat on the floor. Place one or both hands under your lower back (palms facing down) and contract your abdominals and pelvic floor until you feel your back press against your hands. Maintaining this pressure, slowly lift one foot a few inches off the floor, pause, then lower it. Now lift the other foot and continue to alternate until you lose the pressure against your hands.

5 Top gear

Walking is an activity for which very little specialist equipment is needed, but don't let me stop you going on a spending spree! The most important kit is what you put on your feet, so this chapter begins by looking at footwear. We'll then look at clothing and useful gear and gadgets.

Footwear

With 26 bones joined by 37 joints, the foot is a highly complex piece of machinery, worthy of your care and attention. Since a force equal to four times your body weight emanates through the heel each time your foot lands, it is important that your footwear offers adequate support and cushioning. According to a report by Nike, the feet of a 70 kg person carry around 2520 tonnes of load (equivalent to four Eurostar trains) during a typical day, the foot striking the ground 1125 times for each kilometre walked.

During gait (the name given to the walking action), the foot lands in a supinated (arched) position but immediately begins to pronate to facilitate shock absorption. As the foot starts to push the body forward, the foot arches again so that it becomes a rigid lever.

The ideal shoe will enhance shock absorption without hampering the natural movement of the foot. The heel of a walking shoe is lower than that of a running shoe, and doesn't flare out at the back

> **Walking to work allows me time to relax and think, and doesn't add too much time onto my day.**
>
> *Jenny, from Maidstone*

like a running shoe (this aids stability, which isn't necessary in walking). In fact, the heel may even be undercut at the back to allow for a smooth roll through from heel to toe.

A roomy toe box allows the natural splaying of the toes as the fore-foot flexes to push off – a tapered toebox is liable to cause blisters. A cutaway section at the Achilles tendon (at the back of the ankle) is also useful, so that the tendon does not get rubbed or inflamed. The midsole of the walking shoe will be lower than that of a running shoe and the forefoot needs to be more flexible, since in walking, the forefoot tends to strike the ground at a 45-degree angle, compared to running, where it is closer to 30 degrees.

Shopping for shoes

So, where do you start? Try to buy your walking footwear from a specialist shop where the staff can give you advice on models to try. They will probably ask you a few questions to determine the right shoe to meet your needs, so think about the following points:

Questions to consider

- How often will you be walking?
- How heavy are you?
- Where will you be walking? What sort of terrain and climate?
- Do you have any existing foot problems or biomechanical problems?
- What socks will you be wearing?
- Is walking your main/only form of exercise?

How to buy right

- Choose shoes in the afternoon when feet are at their maximum size.
- Lace them up standing up, not sitting (that's how you'll be walking in them).
- Allow for a space as wide as your thumb in the toe box.

- Get your feet measured – but don't be too swayed by what size you think you are supposed to be. Comfort is paramount.
- Don't settle for 'OK'. Gone are the days when you had to 'break' shoes in and suffer all the blisters and pain of doing so.
- Try them on with the type of socks you will be wearing.
- Walk around in them – don't just stand there!

Can't I wear running shoes?

Running shoes are adequate, but most experts recommend buying a walking-specific trainer if this is going to be your primary or sole form of exercise. If you can't find dedicated walking trainers, running ones are the next best thing, but there are some subtle differences. Cross-trainers are generally too inflexible for fitness walking.

Lacing techniques

The way you lace your shoes can subtly alter the fit. A foot that slides back and forth is a foot that is going to end up with blisters and hard skin. If your foot, particularly the heel, is slipping, try a loop-lacing lock to create a secure, more snug fit. Lace up to the second hole till last, then thread the lace through the next hole on its same side, to create a loop. Now thread the other lace through that loop and pull tight. Never over-tighten laces, as this can put stress on the delicate connective tissues in the feet.

The case for going barefoot

Our feet are our contact point with the earth. And yet we cover them in highly cushioned, protective surfaces and consequently, lose a lot of our awareness and sensory feedback. Walking barefoot – providing the surface is safe – is a good way of 'reconnecting' with the earth and rediscovering the muscles in your feet. This in turn can lead to a lower incidence of lower leg injuries, such as plantar fascitis (see page 97) and ankle sprains. Try to spend at least some time in your bare feet and try some of the exercises in the *Happy feet workout* on page 99 to get your tootsies into tip-top shape!

Looking after your shoes

Your walking footwear will last much longer if you look after it properly, so don't squash your feet in your shoes without untying the laces (you'll break down the heel cup), don't stick trainers in the washing machine, don't leave them languishing in the hall covered in mud, don't stick them on the radiator to dry, and wear them only for the purpose you bought them for. If your shoes are wet or dirty, wipe them with a damp cloth and allow them to dry naturally. It's also a good idea to lift the insole out to aid drying.

Another good tip is to buy two pairs of walking trainers, and rotate them. This allows the EVA, the material that forms the mid-sole, to restore itself to its normal shape after continual flattening. Shoes will remain supportive for 300–500 miles – don't rely on the upper to give signs of wear, it is the supportive material in the mid-sole that counts. Boots should be treated the same, but after drying wet leather boots or shoes, treat them with conditioning cream to prevent cracking.

These boots were made for walking

It's a popular myth that you need to endure miles of misery before walking boots are comfortable. Not so. Invest in good quality boots that fit right and you can kiss sore feet – not to mention ankles and shins – goodbye. That said, if you plan to do most of your walking on even, stable surfaces like pavements, you would do better to stick to a walking shoe like those described above. If, however, you will be heading 'off-road' to walk regularly, or plan to make long hikes part of your walking programme, boots are best.

So what are you looking for? Sole flexibility is sacrificed for durability and protection underfoot, so expect a more rigid sole, with a very rugged outsole to give good traction on slippery or uneven terrain, and a reinforced toe-box to protect your toes from rocks and tree roots. A boot that supports the ankle is best for rutted, unstable trails, so that you don't turn your ankle – but make sure the fabric inside is well padded to prevent chafing, and that the tongue isn't so long that it rubs your shin bone when you flex your foot. Whether to opt for leather or a synthetic fibre is a matter of choice – leather boots are heavier, but may be more durable – and if you are going to be walking in wet conditions regularly, it may be worth spending extra money for Gore-tex, which is both lightweight and waterproof.

Get the right fit

Stand up with the boots on both feet, unlaced. Push your toes forward until they touch the front of the boot. If you can fit your index finger easily between your heel and the back of the boot, then you've got the right size.

Barefoot in shoes – the anti-shoe

Recent years have seen a trend for designing shoes that 'mimic' the bare foot. The pioneer in this market was Masai Barefoot Technology (MBT) shoes – Nike recently released the first athletic shoe in the field, the Nike Free. The idea is that the sole of the shoe is slightly unstable and soft, to make the muscles in the foot and calf work much harder, by having to respond to the information they are getting through the soles of the feet. So instead of supporting the feet, the curved, multi-layered sole activates the muscles, rather like the way walking on soft sand does. Even the flattest, hardest surface becomes a more challenging, unstable surface to walk on. The theory is that this also challenges core stability, having a positive effect on posture.

Walking socks

They seem innocent enough, but socks can make or break the comfort of your feet in activity. According to the American Academy of Podiatric Sports Medicine, ill-fitting or inappropriate fabric socks can cause infections, blisters, black toenails and even contribute to the wearing away of the 'fat pads' that cushion the feet.

It is pointless spending good money on a pair of quality shoes or boots, and then wearing a pair of cotton socks from a bargain pack of three. Socks can assist with moisture control, cushioning, temperature and comfort. By investing in a pair of good quality socks, with flat or no seams to chafe, additional padding on the main points of contact and some kind of temperature and moisture control fabrics, you are well on your way to happy feet.

Though your mum might have always told you to stick to natural fabrics, cotton socks retain three times the moisture of acryclic ones, and 14 times the moisture of CoolMax. With the feet producing as much as half a pint of moisture a day each, it is very important that your socks are able to wick moisture from the skin and get rid of it. That's why it is also important to have a breathable upper in the shoe, or at least a shoe liner with 'hydrophilic' fibres. The other problem with cotton is that when wet, it becomes shapeless, leading to bunching and wrinkling – and after a few washes, cotton fibre socks can become hard and abrasive. If you are plagued with blisters, replacing cotton socks with CoolMax or ThorLo is your first strategy. Another good option is to try double-layer socks (two thin layers rather than one single layer) in which the outer layer moves with the shoe while the inner layer stays with the foot, thus eliminating friction on the skin and reducing wear.

> **I started walking after a sports injury. Although at first it seemed quite frustrating, I soon started to enjoy it. I still walk much more that I used to.**
>
> *Chris, from Birmingham*

If your feet are always cold and clammy, alpaca or mohair wool socks are a good bet, while if they get hot, a synthetic blend like CoolMax will wick sweat and keep them drier. If smelly feet are your problem, look for socks with anti-bacterial treatment – such as the addition of X-static silver thread fibres. Natural wool fibre socks are still preferable for hiking because wool has a remarkable ability to maintain heat when wet. But 100 per cent wool can be abrasive, so often wool is blended with high-tech synthetic fibres to give the best of both worlds.

Walking wear

You can walk in anything you find comfortable that doesn't restrict your movement, but if you are going to be walking at pace that makes you hot and sweaty (and I hope you are at some point!) then you may want to opt for fabrics that are breathable and can manage moisture to keep you dry and cool. The best option is to dress in layers so that you can easily adjust your temperature by removing or adding a layer.

The base layer, closest to your skin (which may be all you need in warm weather) should wick moisture from your skin to prevent it from chilling you and also to prevent chafing. This is the layer that should have the snuggest fit. A second layer adds insulation by creating a layer of warm air between the two fabric surfaces. This top should fit more loosely than the base layer. If necessary, an outer layer comes next, which protects you from wind, rain and cold, while still allowing perspiration to evaporate and not linger. A lightweight shower-proof jacket is ideal – especially one that packs away into itself and can be carried easily. Look for ventilation on this garment, such as underarm and back vents, to allow the lower layers to do their jobs.

As for the bottom half, since the legs don't sweat so much as the torso, you don't need to be so particular – a pair of breathable tights, leggings or shorts is perfect.

For hotter days...

In sunnier climes, you may want to replace your base layer with a vest or tank top. Remember also to protect yourself against the sun's rays. There is now a sun protection lotion which you put on once in the morning and don't need to reapply again all day (see Resources). A godsend for us pale and interesting types! Sunglasses are also crucial to protect your eyes from harmful UV rays and to stop you squinting – and to keep flies and grit out your eyes. Normal sunglasses are not ideal as they tend to slip off the nose when you sweat – sports sunglasses will have a 'sticky' nose-bridge, a wraparound design, full UVA and UVB protection and will be shatterproof. They also create a 'barrier' between you and the world, which is a good thing if you find exercising in public intimidating or embarrassing.

I don't recommend a hat to shield you from the sun, since it will conserve heat that could otherwise escape through the head, but a visor is a good way of getting extra shielding without making you feel hotter.

And in the cold and wet...

If you have already opted for base, insulating and outer layers and still feel chilly, consider swapping a lightweight waterproof for a fleece-lined jacket, which provides some protection against wind and rain as well as extra insulation. Don't neglect to cover your extremities in cold weather, too. When you are exercising in the cold, blood is shunted away from these areas to insulate the internal organs and fuel the working muscles. A fleece hat really helps you conserve body heat, and mittens or gloves are also a must.

Top gear

Trekking poles

Poles can be a useful aid to an efficient walking technique, and the extra muscle power provided by the upper body can enable you to travel faster, as well as work the arms, shoulders and chest. They are particularly useful in enhancing balance on tricky descents – research from the University of Salzburg found that they reduced pressure on the knees – and on flatter ground they can improve rhythm. Look out for poles that are telescopic (collapsible) in order to get the length just right and so that you can pack them away when you aren't using them. You also want either aluminium, titanium or carbon fibre poles, as these are lightweight but robust.

Pedometers

A pedometer is perhaps the most useful piece of equipment you can invest in for your walking fitness programme. They are cheap, simple to set up and use, and unobtrusive to wear. The basic function of a pedometer is simply to count the number of steps you take, by detecting vibration (movement) at the hip and recording the information. Many models also allow you to enter the length of your stride, and will then calculate how far (in miles or kilometres) you

The sports bra – a girl's best friend

Walking may be a low-impact activity, but that doesn't mean that a sports bra isn't essential, what ever your bust size. Insufficient – or no – support during movement can result in stretched Cooper's ligaments (the connective tissue that covers the breasts and 'holds' it all together), which will not go back to their normal length, leaving breasts sagging and sometimes sore. A study in the *Journal of Science and Medicine in Sport* found that a designated sports bra reduced both the absolute vertical movement and the maximum downward deceleration force on the breast far more effectively than a crop top or normal bra. It also reduced the incidence of exercise-related breast pain. Other research (albeit by a bra company) has found that a sports bra can reduce breast movement by 56 per cent.

These days, not all sports bras are akin to instruments of torture that you need to strap yourself into. For smaller-chested women, the best style is usually a compression bra that literally presses the breasts against the chest wall. For bigger busts, an encapsulated bra, that supports each breast separately, is usually more appropriate.

Choosing the right bra

- Comfort and fit come first. The bra should be snug but not so tight that it restricts your breathing. It should be level all the way round, not riding up at the back.

- The straps should be wide enough to give proper support and not dig into your skin, but soft enough not to chafe. They should also be adjustable, as the fabric will stretch over time.

- As with all sports kit, cotton isn't ideal. Technical fabrics like Coolmax or Supplex wick sweat so that your body stays dry and comfortable and you avoid chafing.

- If your breasts noticeably change size throughout your menstrual cycle, you may need to consider buying sports bras in different sizes to suit the time of the month.

have walked. Others will also estimate energy expenditure, using information about your weight and size, and distance travelled.

A report by the President's Council on Physical Fitness and Sports concluded that while pedometers were an excellent motivational and useful device for step-counting, the information provided on distance covered and calorie expenditure was not always accurate.

For one thing your stride length changes when you walk on hills – up or down – so unless your route is totally flat, the distance reading may be misleading. To find out if your pedometer is counting correctly, wear it and walk a short distance, counting the number of steps you take in your head. Then compare it to the reading given. An error margin of 5 per cent is considered acceptable.

Bags and belts

You don't want to be holding on to water bottles, maps or other paraphernalia when you are out walking, so a rucksack or bum belt that leaves your hands free is ideal. If you opt for a bum bag, make sure that it fits securely on the hips and does not ride up and down. Many models have drinks holders that you can reach without having to pause for breath. For a rucksack, look for one with a breathable and padded back panel so that you don't end up with a huge sweat patch on your back. Straps that are fully adjustable are also essential, so that the bag doesn't ride up and down and chafe. A strap that secures across the chest usually works well in keeping the bag still. Look for a bag with lots of external pockets so that you don't have to keep rummaging through it.

Heart rate monitor

A heart rate monitor consists of an elasticated chest-strap that transmits heart rate data to a wristwatch. A basic model will tell you what your heart rate is at any given moment and records how long you have been exercising, but more advanced models can be programmed with your personal information (such as age, weight, height and sex) and will then calculate what your heart rate should be when you are working at any given intensity (and bleep a warning if you go too hard... or slack off), how many calories you have burned and even estimate your maximal oxygen uptake (a benchmark measure of aerobic fitness). Some even allow you to download all this information on to your computer. A basic model is available these days for around £40.

Distance measuring devices

A digital map reader is a useful gadget that estimates how far you have travelled when you retrace your route on a map. You simply enter the scale of the map and roll the device's tiny wheel around the route you took and you get the information in miles or kilometres. A little more accurate than the old piece of string trick!

But far more accurate (and pricey) is a Global Positioning System (GPS). If you love gadgets, or are training for a specific event for which your mileage and pace are important, these are a worthwhile investment. By receiving information from satellites, a GPS tracking system can monitor your exact speed, pace and distance because it knows exactly where you are. You can also enter grid references for navigation. And at the end of your walk, you can find out what your average pace was, how high you climbed, how far you've travelled, how long it took – and even compare the information to a previous walk.

Let's walk

Walking can lower the risk of some cancers. A large study of 80,000 men and women in Scandinavia found that recreational activity was enough to bring a 40 per cent reduction in the risk of colon cancer among women, although only men who were over 45 at the time the study clearly benefited. But there is better news for the boys: the Honolulu Heart Study, a study of 8000 men, found that over a 12-year period, walking just two miles a day cut the risk of death almost in half. The walkers' risk of death was especially lower from cancer. And for women, a study published in the journal *Epidemiology* found that those who took up exercise after the menopause had a 30 per cent lower risk of developing breast cancer, while those who had been active throughout their lives had a 42 per cent lower risk than sedentary women.

6 Sticking with it

When you first resolve to get fit, you feel full of enthusiasm for your new project. But actually executing it can be a different matter. The thing is, life just seems to get in the way! Well, the good news is that choosing to walk your way to fitness means you will have significantly more opportunities to get your activity in than if you were doing something that was less flexible and practical. But you do still need to think laterally about scheduling regular exercise into your life, and it helps to have a few tricks and tactics to hand for when the going gets tough.

Make it a priority

If you want to enjoy all the benefits of being healthier and fitter then you need to accept that your regular workouts are important – they need to become part of the fabric of your life, rather than merely something you hope you'll be able to fit in. It really helps if you can plan in advance when you are going to fit in your walks during the coming week and make a note of them, just as you would if you had to find the time for a doctor's appointment or business meeting. It also helps to let your nearest and dearest know how important it is for you to get your regular walking fix! If they understand how much it means to you, they will help you find the time to do it and won't be resentful. Even better, persuade them to walk with you! But don't be all or nothing about exercise. Just because you perhaps can't fit in the 90-minute session you had planned, it doesn't mean that it isn't worth doing anything at all – do what you can. Remember, any activity is better than none.

Here are a few ideas on how you can fit walking into your busy life:

- Walk to a business meeting instead of jumping in a taxi or driving – even better, suggest to your colleague that you 'walk and talk'.

- Plan a route with a 'treat' at the end of the walk – such as a great coffee shop where you can enjoy a cappuccino.

- If you and a friend don't seem to have time to catch up or work out, kill two birds with one stone by meeting up for a brisk walk. The continuous conversation will be an added challenge!

- No time for a lunch-time walk? OK, but you could walk to a sandwich shop further away from work to get at least some additional steps in.

- Use your time creatively – if you have to drop the kids off at swimming club and normally hang around waiting for them, go for a walk in the interim and pick them up afterwards. Or if you have clothes in the launderette, walk while they are washing – you can then do your stretches while they tumble-dry.

- Walk around the perimeter of the play area while the kids are playing – walk with the dog instead of standing still and throwing sticks or balls.

- Shorten your journeys on public transport by getting on or off the train or bus somewhere that allows you to fit in some walking.

- Always be ready for a walk if the opportunity arises – have appropriate footwear and clothing in your car, your office drawer or wherever it may be handy for an impromptu session.

> **Walking really allows you time to take look around you and take in the scenery**
>
> *Colette, from Harrogate*

If motivation wanes...

If you are beginning to lose your enthusiasm for walking, try really hard to pinpoint why. Is it because you are no longer seeing improvements? Or are you bored? Perhaps you aren't getting enough enjoyment from your walking. Here are some tips on kick-starting your motivation.

Go alone

Walking alone can be a profound experience, particularly if you are in beautiful surroundings. Research has shown that due to its repetitive and uncomplicated nature, walking is the perfect type of exercise to allow you to slip into a state of mind that is conducive to problem solving and creative thinking. It's also easier to get into a state of flow if you are alone.

Make it a group effort

If you don't feel happy walking alone, or find it boring, then a walking group may help you stay motivated. It could be just you and a couple of friends, or it could be an official group, with an experienced leader. A personal trainer may also be helpful in showing you how to get more from your walking workout and making you work a little harder than you would on your own. See Resources on page 116.

Go for goals

Maybe you haven't got anything to aim for with your walking. Log your progress. Time yourself on a set route – or try the Rockport Mile test again to see if your time has improved. Wear your pedometer to see whether your daily step count has increased. Or aim high and enroll on a charity walk or walking marathon (see pages 88–9).

Make it meaningful

Perhaps you'd find walking more rewarding if it had a purpose. Raising money for charity, bird watching, spotting spring flowers as they appear, picking up litter are all ways of getting more out of your walk than a workout.

Listen to music

There is scientific evidence to suggest that listening to music can take you out of yourself while you exercise, distracting you from discomfort and boredom, and making the experience more enjoyable. Another bonus is that it reduces your 'perception of effort' so that you unwittingly work at a higher effort level without noticing. The music should ideally be quite upbeat and pacey. Listening to 'I'm not in love' by 10cc is hardly going to have you striding out with a smile on your face.

Do something different

If you normally power walk around your local area, swap one session for a day's hike in a country park. If you are more of a weekend rambler, try a 20-minute threshold walk around the park. If it's all seeming a bit serious, take the kids on a nature trail, run around with Rover, or take a ball to dribble or a Frisbee to throw.

Go with the flow

The US trend for 'wandering' really just means walking with no given plan or route. It is refreshing, mentally and physically, to leave the watch and heart rate monitoring behind and just do what feels right as far as pace, direction and length of session are concerned.

Go green

The 'biophilia' theory states that the presence of natural things – be it trees, rivers, flowers or your pet Yorkshire terrier – makes us feel good. It also states that we have a natural desire for contact with nature. Meanwhile, research suggests that regular activity positively affects mental well-being and self-esteem and can have an antidepressant effect. So putting the two together – exercise and the natural environment – may have doubly positive effects. In a research project conducted by the University of Essex that looked at the effect of 'green exercise' on health, there was a significant improvement in self-esteem in 9 out of 10 projects, alongside physical benefits. Other studies have found a greater mood boost from exercising outdoors compared to exercising on a treadmill.

Keep a journal

People who keep a training log are more consistent with their workouts than those who don't. Your training diary can be as detailed as you like – you could include information about your route, what the weather was like, what you saw on the way, what sort of mood you were in, information about your effort level and pace and distance, or simply put 'walked 45 minutes'. It can be useful to include information about any aches or niggles you have, so that you can keep tabs on whether an injury might be on its way. Take note of your test results from page 11 if you decide to keep a training log and then repeat them at regular intervals to gauge your progress. It's also a good idea to note things like when you bought your trainers, so that you don't inadvertently walk in them for months after they are worn out.

Let's walk

It seems that aerobic exercise, particularly rhythmic, repetitive activities can help you solve problems and think more creatively. Research from the University of Middlesex found that volunteers scored higher on creative thinking tasks after a 25-minute aerobic workout compared to after watching a DVD.

No buts... walking excuses challenged!

'But I'm too tired'

Many people feel that they barely have the energy to get through the day's tasks, let alone have spare energy for regular workouts. But being active on a regular basis actually *increases* your energy levels. Look at it like this – if running for a train or carrying two bags of shopping is tiring, then getting stronger and improving your aerobic fitness will make these activities feel easier. The result is that you expend less energy on these daily activities and don't feel so tired by the end of the day. Plus, of course, you have more energy left for your workout and to plan your healthy meals, rather than grabbing a ready-made meal or takeaway on your way home.

The increase in breathing rate caused by exercise gets more oxygen into your lungs, muscles and brain, and removes waste products such as carbon dioxide, so you end up feeling more alert and less sluggish. It also improves digestion and reduces the time it takes food to pass through the guts. To prove the point, a 2005 study in the journal *Medicine & Science in Sport & Exercise* found a positive association between the amount of typical weekly physical activity reported and the frequency with which people report feeling energetic (vigour and vitality). Randomised controlled experiments even show that exercise training boosts energy in fatigued people with medical conditions. If you're so rushed at the start of the day – or so whacked by the end of it – that exercise simply falls off the agenda, then walking may be the perfect form of activity because you are already doing it – you just need to fine-tune your daily walking and increase it a little.

'But I haven't got time'

This is one of the main reasons given for not starting – or for giving up –an exercise plan. Our lives seem increasingly busy and hectic, but the fact is there are 24 hours in a day and we can all find some spare minutes of that to walk. At least when walking you can use your workout to actually get somewhere, fulfil a task or socialise (unlike swimming up and down a swimming pool or climbing an endless flight of steps to nowhere in the gym). Be creative about how you can fit walking in. Could you walk the kids to school instead of driving (or even drive halfway and then walk)? Could you walk for 20 minutes before you hit the sandwich shop at lunch time? Could you meet a friend and walk and talk instead of going for coffee?

Excitingly, research is beginning to indicate that many of the benefits of extended workouts can be gained from shorter ones, repeated throughout the day. For example, research published in the *Journal of Strength and Conditioning Research* studied the fitness gains from walking for 30 minutes continuously compared to walking for 10 minutes, 3 times during the day. It found that both timescales were beneficial in maintaining aerobic fitness.

The other point to bear in mind regarding lack of time is that it isn't ever going to change! There'll never be more than 24 hours in a day, so if you can't fit it in this week, month or year, what makes you think that you will be able to next year? The point is you need to *take* time, not *make* time.

'But I've tried it before and it didn't work'

Ah, yes! The biggest factor in giving up on any exercise regime is lack of results. And, when I see people out in the parks for their daily 'power walk', I do see why they aren't getting the results they want. You need to get the technique and posture right, you need to walk briskly and you need to increase the challenge progressively as you get fitter, to enjoy continued health, fitness and aesthetic improvements. If you always walk at the same pace, for the same distance, your body will quickly become accustomed to this and, unless you ring the changes, your fitness gains will begin to tail off. Happily, this book will show you exactly how to do all of these things!

'But it's boring'

If you find walking boring, then perhaps you aren't getting enough variety. Do you always walk alone? Try walking with a friend (it's the ideal way to catch up on each other's news), take the children and make it fun by playing games or getting them to collect things, or take the dog. Do you always walk the same routes? Take a train or bus ride somewhere and explore new

> The best thing about walking is that it doesn't require anything apart from comfy shoes
>
> *John, from Walsall*

territory. There are miles of public footpaths and national trails around the UK – you'll get to see some of the finest scenery and immerse yourself in nature for the day. The other reason you may find walking boring is because it isn't challenging enough. If that's the case, then you'll find plenty of ideas on how to make it more of a workout throughout the book.

Ways to walk

Yes, there is more than one way to put one foot in front of the other! Whether you want to walk competitively, try walking in a different environment or just learn something new, read on to find out about some of the best ways to walk

Power walking

Power walking is really just fast walking – a typical speed for a power walker is 5 mph. The speed comes from two things – a short, fast stride with a strong 'toe-off', and powerful use of the arms. In power walking, the arms are bent to 90-degrees, close to your sides, and move forward and back vigorously enough to propel you forward. In fact, as your fitness walking technique improves, it is likely that you will instinctively adopt the stance of a power walker, as it is easier to propel yourself forward at speed with arms bent and a short, swift stride. Some athletics clubs have power-walking sections, and although it hasn't become the massive activity it is in the United States, there are enough power walkers out there for you not to feel silly in the park. See *Resources* for details.

Hiking

Hiking as a form of walking is more a matter of place than of technique. It immediately conjures up images of rugged landscapes, sweeping views and undulating terrain. Covering terrain that may be wet, muddy, rocky or unstable means that you won't be able to maintain a steady pace during a long hike – don't try to. The goal is to try for an even effort, so that you speed up when the going is good and slow down on lung-busting ascents or tricky descents. You will need robust footwear, comfortable clothing and a backpack roomy enough to carry water and food, protection against the weather (such as sunscreen, a hat or a waterproof) and maps. Think about going on a navigation course if your map-reading skills are a little rusty! You can read about boots and equipment on pages 65–75 and find out more about hiking routes, groups and kit in *Resources* on page 116–19.

Orienteering

Though normally considered a running activity, orienteering is another way of getting off the beaten track and enjoying a demanding walking workout. The idea of orienteering is to follow a set of clues, known as 'controls', using a map and compass in as short a time as possible before returning to the start line with your card punched to prove you found all the controls. The level of difficulty is colour-coded, so you won't be competing against people far more experienced than you. It is a lot of fun, and speed isn't the only factor in success. There are some permanent Orienteering courses in the UK, and regular beginner-friendly events. See *Resources* for more information.

Race walking

Race walking is a competitive athletic sport, famed for the unique 'wiggle' that is integral to good technique. Race walkers can reach speeds that many of us would be pleased to achieve in running – up to 14 km/h – but research shows that the injury rate among competitive race walkers is much lower than that among elite runners. The Race Walking Association rules state that 'race walking is a progression of steps so taken that the walker makes contact with the ground, so that no visible (to the human eye) loss of contact occurs. The advancing leg shall be straightened (i.e., not bent at the knee) from the moment of first contact with the ground until the vertical upright position.' It is this leg straightness that forces the hips to rotate so visibly, giving the wiggle.

There is an introductory type of race walking designed to help beginners, in which the 'straightening' part of the rule is not applied; only continuous contact with the ground is required, which is what distinguishes the activity from running. Race walkers recommend mastering the technique first, and then working on speed. It is still a tiny sport in the UK – not much more than 2200 people take part in events (which range from 1 mile to 100) – but many more race walk for the health and fitness benefits. See *Resources* for information on clubs and events.

Nordic Walking

While still relatively unknown in the UK, Nordic Walking is a huge sport in northern Europe. It simply involves walking with special poles (not the same as trekking poles) to increase energy expenditure, and has been described as 'cross-country skiing without the skis or snow!' It originated as a summer training programme for cross-country skiers, so it's no surprise that it works the body harder than normal walking. Research in the journal *Research Quarterly for Exercise and Sport* found that heart rate tends to be 5–17 bpm higher due to the use of the muscles of the upper body (the back, chest, shoulders and arms). Energy expenditure is as much as 20 per cent higher for the same walking speed. Aficionados also say it is better for the back, as the technique requires greater rotational movement of the spine (the direction of motion that tends to deteriorate first). And although you are using more muscles and working harder, the effort is spread across your whole body and, therefore, Nordic Walking can actually feel easier and less tiring than normal walking, say its supporters.

Nordic Walking poles differ from trekking poles in that they are single-piece construction (rather than being adjustable, and therefore collapsible). They can bend without snapping, and have specially designed hand straps, which allow you to release the grip as you push forward, reducing neck and shoulder tension.

> **Walking allows me to keep my weight down, and it's so easy that I hardly notice that I am doing it! I find it is certainly the best way to exercise.**
>
> *Sue, from Surrey*

Walk like a Norwegian

- Walk naturally. Nordic Walking is an enhancement of normal walking, not a different movement.
- Keep your shoulders relaxed.
- Lean slightly forwards.
- Hands and poles remain close to your body.

- As your right foot moves forward, so does your left hand, and vice versa.
- Allow the sole of your foot to roll from your heel to the ball of your foot.
- Try to maintain the pole thrust behind the line of your pelvis.
- At the end of the pole thrust open your palms slightly and push into the strap. This creates a greater stretch of your arm and greater spinal rotation. With correct Nordic Walking technique there is a clear swing of your shoulders and hips.
- Bring the pole forward with the grip first, not the tip end first. The pole tip remains behind the line of your body (don't plant the poles in front of you).
- Stretch your body gently at the end of your walk.
- Try a slight incline if you are finding it hard to master the technique. This makes it easier to get the movement correct.

Indoor walking

For many of us, half the fun of a walking programme is getting outdoors, but when the weather is terrible, or time or place constraints prevent you from walking safely or comfortably outside, there is always the great indoors. In the United States, 'mall walking' is a popular activity – groups of walkers get together and stride out around shopping malls. There are also 'indoor walking' exercise videos available, that effectively turn the space in front of your television set into a makeshift walking track. A range of walking steps (marching in place, forwards, back and side stepping) are usually mixed with other lower body moves such as squats and lunges (see *Resources*). And then there is the treadmill.

The treadmill can be a valuable training tool – not only does it excuse you from walking in inclement weather, it can also provide a very precise and controlled workout. For example, you may be doing an interval session outside, and without realising, your speed on each interval is gradually dropping as you get tired. On the treadmill, however, this would quickly become apparent and you have to put a little extra effort in to maintain your speed. The gradient function also allows you to incorporate hills into any walk. Try to keep your walking style as natural as possible on the treadmill – use your arms (don't hold the rails!) and try to maintain your usual stride length.

Buying a treadmill

If you've got the space and budget you might consider buying your own treadmill. You'll need to spend at least £1000 if you want something that will be durable and efficient. Don't rush in, and don't buy anything that you haven't tested first. Think about the following points:

- How much space will it take up?
- Where will you put it? A dingy garage won't be very inviting!
- Has it got a gradient function; does it go downhill as well as up?
- Is the belt smooth – and is it long and wide enough for your stride?
- Is the action quiet?
- Do you get a decent service/maintenance contract?

Events and races

Entering a competitive walk is a sure-fire way of keeping your mind focused on your training! If you don't fancy race walking, there are hundreds of road and trail races throughout the UK. Though primarily aimed at runners, many are 'walker-friendly'. Events such as the 5 km Race for Life series (a nationwide network of events for women only) positively welcome walkers. If getting a good time in a race isn't sufficient incentive, think about raising money for a charity by getting sponsors – some charities actually organise annual sponsored walks.

Walk the Walk, the charity set up by Nina Barough to raise money and awareness for breast cancer research, has got thousands of women taking part in designated power walking events in their bras.

Walk the Walkers take part in races from 5km to marathon distance (the charity organises the famous MoonWalk Marathon in London), and offers training groups to help you achieve your goals.

If you want to push the boundaries even further than a marathon, you may consider tackling a long distance path, such as the South West Coast Path or Pennine Way, or signing up for a multi-day event, such as a trek around the Himalaya or along the Inca Trail. Many charities offer such trips for a minimum guaranteed amount of funds raised. See *Resources* on page 117 for details.

Walking holidays and breaks

Another way of injecting some variety into your walking regime is to go on a walking break or holiday. You can design and plan your own and carry everything you'll need in a backpack, opt for a self-guided walk, in which your luggage is transported from place to place for you, or join a guided group. Some companies offer themed holidays, such as wine, bird-watching or natural history based trips. Walking is a fantastic way of seeing a country – yours or a foreign land – as you get a chance to experience the scenery, people and culture at a pace at which you can take it all in. If you are a fairly new regular walker, it might pay to start by going on an organised trip so that you don't bite off more than you can chew! See *Resources* on pages 117–18 for some ideas on who to contact.

7 Avoiding danger and injury

From strangers to aggressive dogs to slippery trails and thunderstorms… there are inevitably going to be a few risks to contend with when your workout takes place outside the confines of a health club. Walking with a friend, partner or group can minimise the threat to your personal safety, particularly for women, but it isn't always practical or possible to walk with others. So it is wise to take a few sensible precautions when you are walking alone.

Safety first

- Always know where you are and where the nearest point of 'civilisation' is.
- Stay aware. Don't walk wearing a radio or personal stereo as you won't be alert to potential dangers from people or traffic. Keep music for the treadmill.
- Don't be too proud to ask for directions if you get lost! Ideally, ask a passer-by rather than someone in a car.
- Walk with an air of confidence but don't be confrontational – keep your eyes neutral – neither avoiding nor seeking contact with others.
- In winter, I wear a woolly hat with my hair tucked inside and a loose top or jacket so that I could pass for male or female.

- Let someone know where you're going and how long you think you will be – if you live alone, leave a message on someone's answer phone.

- Consider carrying your mobile phone in a bum bag, backpack or pocket, or a coin for making a phone call from a public call box or even jumping on a bus.

- Vary your routes and the time at which you walk. It's just possible that someone may take note of the fact that you are always in a particular place at that time and act upon it.

- Stick to well-lit areas after dark and try to walk where there are plenty of other people, such as a park full of joggers and dog walkers.

- Trust your intuition. If something doesn't feel right, then it probably isn't – so go with your instinct.

- Consider carrying a personal alarm to give yourself precious seconds to get away if you should be attacked. The Train Alarm is palm-sized (no good carrying it in your rucksack where it's not easily accessible) and emits a loud siren when the pin is pulled out.

- You may also consider taking a self-defence class to improve your knowledge of what to do should you ever get attacked.

- Carry a slip of paper under the sole of your shoe with your name, telephone number and blood type on, plus any other relevant medical information (allergies, etc.).

Dealing with dogs... and other four-legged foe

Unless you always walk on pavements, you are bound to be in places where dogs are loose. If a dog starts to chase you, slow down or stop and it will almost certainly lose interest; but don't stare at it if it's growling. If a dog jumps up at you say, 'No' or 'Down' firmly. If you have to pass through a property, such as a farm, with a loose dog, try to keep as far away from the dog as you can and don't make eye contact. But also avoid startling dogs – or any animals for that matter – by making them aware of your approach.

On country walks, avoid walking through the midst of livestock, keep to the outside of the field if possible, and keep as much distance as possible if there are young around.

Always follow the Countryside Code, shutting gates and respecting rights of way signs. If you are walking in long grass, consider wearing long pants rather than shorts to reduce the risk of getting a tick, which can cause Lyme's disease. If you have been walking in undergrowth, always check yourself (and your dog) when you return home for signs of ticks – if you find one, don't pull it straight out but twist it out in an anti-clockwise direction, or seek medical advice.

Walking in extreme temperatures

The idea of walking in the snow may sound rather unappealing now, but the chances are you'll be so used to your regular walking workouts that you'll still want to go even when the weather is less than perfect. If you are planning a long walk, it's wise to check the weather forecast before you set off so that you are prepared for any change. You can enter a postcode to get a 5-day forecast at www.bbc.co.uk/weather.

In very hot conditions, the advice on wearing technical, breathable fabrics is even more important – as is protecting your eyes with sunglasses and your skin with a strong sun protection factor. You will also need to be extra vigilant about drinking, as you will dehydrate far more quickly in warmer climes. For longer walks, you could freeze one of your water bottles the day before you go, so that the fluid takes a few hours to melt and you get a cool drink when you are on the move.

On cold days, your fingers, toes and nose are vulnerable to frostbite, so wear a hat and gloves, and perhaps even a scarf. Follow the tips below if you are walking on a cold day:

- Warm up before you leave the house and consider warming up for longer.
- Eat before you set off, particularly if it is to be a long walk – you need to insulate yourself against the cold.
- Don't neglect hydration. You may not feel as if you are sweating, but once you're on the move, you certainly will be.

- If you are on a long walk, bear in mind that your body temperature won't be as high as it is during a short sharp session, so dress accordingly.
- Watch your footing in icy conditions. Make sure your shoes or boots have sufficient traction.

If you get caught in a storm when you are out walking, do not stand under a tree until it has passed. Anything that protrudes high above the ground, such as a tree or power line, is a likely target for lightning. If you are in an exposed place with no cover, crouch down low on the ground, and if you are high up, try to get somewhere lower.

> **The only real downside to walking is the weather. I have found that a good, breathable waterproof coat has solved all my problems!**
>
> *Jill, from Canterbury*

Ailments and injuries

Providing you build up your walking programme gradually, warm up, cool down and stretch, and look where you are going, injury won't be a high risk! But here are a few of the occupational hazards regular walkers may encounter, and what to do about them.

Achilles tendinitis

This is inflammation, pain and tenderness along the Achilles tendon at the back of the lower leg, which attaches the calf muscles to the heel bone. It is often caused by doing too much, too soon instead of building training up gradually, although tight calf muscles and inappropriate footwear can also be to blame, for example, an inflexible sole, or a raised heel tab, which can repeatedly rub the tendon and cause inflammation. The first port of call is the RICED treatment (see pages 98–9). The exercises on pages 54 and 56 will also help enhance strength and flexibility in the lower leg. Heel supports in the shoe may be necessary to reduce stress on the tendon.

Ankle sprain

Turning your ankle or uneven terrain is an occupational hazard when you are a walker! And if you have ever sprained your ankle before, or have particularly weak ankles, then you are more at risk. If you do sprain your ankle, get RICED as soon as possible and see a doctor to ensure no bones are broken or ligaments ruptured. You will need to rest for at least a week – maybe far longer if the sprain is severe. The important bit is rehabilitation, as unless you re-train yourself to move the ankle freely in all directions and to bear weight confidently, you are susceptible to a repeat sprain. A wobble board can help strengthen the muscles of the lower legs and prevent reoccurrence, and try the exercises on pages 54 and 56.

Athlete's foot

Athlete's foot is a fungal infection that loves damp, sweaty places, like trainers and smelly boots! If you are prone to this painful and itchy condition, try dabbing tea tree oil between your toes after you have thoroughly washed and dried them and wear flip-flops if you are in public, wet areas, such as shower blocks or gym changing rooms. An attack can be curbed by using an anti-fungal product, such as Lamisil or Daktarin – but remember, your trainers or boots may be harbouring the culprit: soak the insoles in a tea tree oil solution or spray with an anti-fungal spray.

Blisters

Blisters are a build-up of fluid between the upper and lower layers of the skin, caused by friction between you and your shoes or socks. Good-fitting shoes and socks can go a long way towards preventing them. But if you get a blister, protect it from further friction with a blister plaster, moleskin or even surgical tape. You only need to burst it if it feels painful or if it is hampering your training. If you do decide to pop it, then use a sterilised needle, heated in a flame, and pop it close to the unblistered skin to drain the fluid. Dab antiseptic lotion on and then cover with a blister plaster for at least 48 hours before leaving bare. Always have a stash of blister plasters handy. Look for those that create a 'second skin' between the blister and your footwear, such as Compeed or Hydra-Gel, to cushion the skin. These are also breathable and waterproof, so your blister won't fester or get sore.

Bruised toenails

Black toenails are the result of bruising and blood blisters under the nail, normally caused by your toes repeatedly hitting the front of your shoe. Shoes that are too tight, or too big, can cause this – as can continuous stretches of walking downhill. If the toenail just looks ugly and doesn't hurt, leave it alone. It will either grow out or, more likely, fall off. If, however, there is a soreness and pressure behind the nail, you may need to drain the blood blister by piercing the nail. It is best to get a podiatrist or doctor to do this for you.

Corns and calluses

Contrary to popular belief, corns don't have a root. They are simply a hard-packed layer of dead skin cells that have been caused by repeated pressure on a particular area of the foot. A corn plaster will relieve the pressure, but a chiropodist will be able to get rid of the hard skin for you and advise you on keeping them at bay. The most common cause of corns and calluses is poorly-fitting shoes or boots, but if they keep reappearing in the same place, it can be a telltale sign that your biomechanics are slightly off-kilter, causing either the medial or lateral edge of the foot to undergo more pressure. If this is the case, it is likely that you would also be experiencing niggling pains or aches in the ankles, knees, hips or back.

Cramp

Cramp – either during or after your workout – is most common in muscles that cross more than one joint, such as the gastrocnemius muscle in the calf, which crosses the ankle and knee, and the biceps femoris, which crosses the hip and knee. It can also occur in the feet. Stretching the muscle is one of the best solutions, according to research from Cape Town University in South Africa, which revealed that fatigue caused muscles to contract in a haphazard, involuntary fashion. If you can bear it, massaging the cramping area can also help alleviate the pain. Cramp can also be caused by dehydration, not just through loss of fluid but also of electrolytes – potassium and sodium salts – in the blood. Ensure your diet has sufficient potassium (bananas, potatoes and dried apricots are all good sources), or experiment with isotonic sports drinks during your walks to remedy the problem.

Metatarsalgia

This is an umbrella term for pain or aching in the metatarsal bones in the foot. It can be caused by under-supportive footwear or tight-fitting shoes that don't allow the natural stretching of the toes as the foot flexes. Morton's neuroma is a form of metatarsalgia in which the tissue surrounding a nerve becomes inflamed, causing a burning or tingling sensation and cramping in the forefoot; it can also be caused by tight or ill-fitting shoes, injury or abnormal bone structure. See a podiatrist if you experience tingling or aching pain in the feet during or after walking.

Plantar fascitis

The plantar fascia is a wide, fibrous band that stretches from the heel to the ball of the foot and helps to absorb shock, as well as supporting the arches of the foot. Plantar fascitis is when small tears and inflammation occur, usually at the attachment to the heel bone, causing a pain that can radiate all the way along the sole of the foot. It is more common in people with tight Achilles tendons and those who are overweight, but unsupportive footwear can also cause it. Most people with plantar fascitis experience pain in the heel with their first steps in the morning, as the fascia tightens overnight.

Apply the RICED protocol at the first sign of pain, and arrange to see a physiotherapist for appropriate exercises, stretching and massage, as this can be a stubborn condition to get rid of.

Shin splints (tibial stress syndrome)

Shin splints is the name given to a number of conditions which affect the lower leg – the more correct name for conditions in which there is inflammation of the connective tissue or 'fascia', which attaches to the main shinbone (the tibia), is tibial stress syndrome.

This is most common in beginners, whose lower leg muscles are unaccustomed to exercise, and in people who walk too much on hard surfaces. The telltale sign is a dull or throbbing ache along the front of the shin (anterior tibial stress syndrome), or the inner side of the lower leg (medial tibial stress syndrome), just where the muscle and bone meet. The exercises on pages 54 and 56, a thorough warm-up, cool down and stretch and appropriate footwear will minimise the risk. If a very specific area of soreness is present, it could be a stress fracture, a tiny hairline crack in the bone, caused by repeated impact, but this is more common in runners.

Another shin condition, known as compartment syndrome, is characterised by generalised shin pain that always comes on at the same time or distance into your run. This is because compartment syndrome is caused by the muscles swelling within the sheath-like 'fascia' of the shin, with a resultant increase in pressure to the point at which the structures are pressing against the shin bone and blood flow is compromised. The symptoms include leg pain, unusual nerve sensations (paresthesia) and muscle weakness. If a compartment syndrome is suspected, see a doctor straight away – the RICED protocol will not help.

Stitches

If you get a stitch while you are out walking, try massaging in to the sore area while breathing deeply, or bend fully forwards. Slowing down to a conversation pace usually alleviates the problem. Unbelievably, the wonders of modern science still haven't fathomed out why we get stitches. Researchers from the University of Newcastle in Australia suggest eating small amounts of food rather than big meals, avoiding foods high in sugar and fat just before a workout and also steering clear of some specific foods, including apples, fruit juice, dairy products and chocolate. They also advise not skimping on the warm-up!

How to get RICED properly
RICED stands for rest, ice, compression, elevation and drugs. It is the first 'port of call' for any musculoskeletal injury involving swelling, inflammation, redness or heat.

Rest means no stress on the injured part for 24–48 hours, not trying it every 10 minutes to see if it's better.

Ice can really help reduce inflammation and swelling. Apply crushed ice or use frozen peas or sweetcorn rather than rigid icepacks or cubes. Don't put it directly on your skin – use cling-film or muslin. Ice for 15 minutes every hour for the first few hours, then 15 minutes every two hours – or if that isn't practical, as often as you can. For best results, apply ice along with compression – so pack the ice inside an elastic bandage, for example. This all helps reduce blood flow to the injured part.

If it's practical, elevate the 'sore bit' above your heart.

The D stands for drugs. If your injury involves swelling, redness or heat, you are looking for a non-steroidal anti-inflammatory such as aspirin or ibuprofen, but never use for more than about a week and NEVER use drugs to enable you to mask pain while you train.

The happy feet workout

Give your feet a mini-workout while you're watching TV – strong, flexible feet are less problem-prone. Also, try to spend at least some of your time in bare feet so they don't have to rely entirely on shoes for support and protection.

- With your foot on the floor, rise up on to your toes, and then curl the toes over. Repeat 10 times and hold each position for 5 seconds.
- Place toe separators between your toes and squeeze them for 5 seconds.
- Place a thick rubber band around both big toes and pull them away from each other. Hold for 5 seconds and repeat 10 times.
- Towel curls. Place a towel on the floor and curl it towards you using only your toes. Repeat 5 times.
- Put a golf ball under the ball of your foot and roll it around.
- Write your name in the air with your big toe as 'the pen' by moving the foot and ankle.

8 Nutrition and hydration

With so much conflicting information out there about *what* we should and should not eat, *when* we should and should not eat and *how much* we should eat, it's no wonder many of us are confused about how to eat healthily. Let's get one thing straight: there is no such thing as good and bad foods – just good and bad diets. So you don't have to vow to never eat chocolate, white bread, ice cream or the skin off the roast chicken ever again – healthy eating is simply a matter of getting the balance right and ensuring your diet is varied.

The ideal diet for a regularly active person contains plenty of carbohydrate – 55–65 per cent of total calories – with 15–17 per cent from protein and 20–25 per cent from fat. The average person consumes too much fat (the average is the UK is just under 39 per cent) and too little carbohydrate, which is not only bad news for fuelling workouts but also for controlling body weight.

Food for fuel

Most foods are not made up exclusively of one type of fuel but contain a mixture, say of carbohydrate and protein (like beans) or protein and fat (like meat). The overall energy content (kcal value) of a food is the sum total of each component it contains. Providing the total number of calories you consume doesn't exceed the number that you burn off through daily living and your workouts, you will maintain a healthy weight. It's only when you either consume too many or burn too few that weight creeps – or piles – on!

How much do you need?

To get an estimate of how many calories you need, grab a calculator and do the following sums:

1. My weight in kilograms (1 kilogram = 2.2 lbs).
2. Carry out the following sums:

FEMALES

I am 18–30 years old: weight x 14.7. Answer + 496 =RMR **or**
I am 31–60 years old: weight x 8.7. Answer + 829 = RMR

MALES

I am 18–30 years old: weight x 15.3. Answer + 679 = RMR **or**

I am 31–60 years old: weight x 11.6. Answer + 879 = RMR
MY ESTIMATED RMR IS _____

3. Take this figure and multiply it by the number below most closely representing your typical daily activity level.

I am sedentary (sit or stand most of the day)   **1.4**
I am moderately active (some walking each day and regular active leisure time activities)   **1.7**
I am very active (physically active each day)   **2.0**

MY RESULT IS _____

Losing weight, staying active

Of course, if you want to lose weight, you'll need to consume less than this figure, in order to create a calorie deficit. Alternatively, you can increase the amount of energy expended on exercise by walking more or combining walking with other types of activity. The ideal solution is to cut down your energy intake a little and increase your energy expenditure. That way, you don't have to make enormous life changes but you will, in time, get the results you want. Aim to cut your daily calories by 15 per cent – this will ensure you still have all the energy you need for exercise while facilitating weight loss.

Getting your diet right

Carbohydrates

Carbohydrate is the body's preferred fuel source – and is the only fuel that the brain can utilise. But carbs come in different 'packages' – those that release their energy slowly, such as brown rice and porridge oats, have what is known as a low glycaemic index (GI), while refined starches, like white bread and rice, cause a sharp rise and fall in blood sugar and have a high glycaemic index. High glycaemic carbohydrates can create energy highs and lows by flooding the blood with insulin, encouraging fat storage, decreasing insulin sensitivity and possibly raising the risk of diabetes. Too many high GI carbs may also cause you to snack unnecessarily or forego workouts because you feel tired, so opt for low GI carbs such as whole grains, pulses, wholemeal pasta, rice and cereal, along with a wide variety of fruits and vegetables (see below). The current trend for low-carbohydrate diets is bad news for active people – as well as providing ready-to-use fuel, carbohydrate-rich foods are also high in B vitamins, fibre and phytochemicals, which can help prevent cancer and promote good health.

> **Walking is accessible to most people, and it doesn't cost much**
>
> *Bill, from Surrey*

Protein

Protein is not one of the body's major fuel suppliers – it prefers to use carbohydrate and fat – but in some situations, such as when the muscle's carbohydrate stores have been used up, or when you aren't consuming enough carbohydrate, protein can be broken down to produce energy, reflecting its role in the body as a 'building block' for muscle and other organs. Unless you are training particularly heavily, you don't need to increase your protein intake – moderately active people are recommended to aim for 0.75–1.2 g per kilo of body weight each day (providing you eat a serving of protein at lunch and dinner, you should be fine). Good quality sources include poultry, lean meat (trim off visible fat and skin), low-fat dairy products, eggs, fish and seafood, tofu, pulses and nuts.

Fats

Not only is the average person's fat consumption too high, the type of fat we eat is often the 'wrong' type, too, coming from unhealthy saturated and trans fat sources (derived from meat and dairy products, pastry, fried and refined 'ready' meals, cakes and biscuits). Healthier fat sources are monounsaturated fats (such as olive oil, rapeseed oil and some nut oils) and the two essential fatty acids, Omega-3 and Omega-6. They are called 'essential' as we are unable to manufacture them in the body. Good sources of Omega 3 include oily fish, flaxseed, hempseed, walnuts and their oils, canola and soybean oils and, to a lesser extent, green leafy vegetables; Omega 6 is derived from seed oils, corn oil, nuts and wheat-germ. Aiming for no more than 10 per cent of total calories from saturated fat and a bare minimum of trans fats will help you maintain a healthy body weight and improve your heart health significantly.

Although the average person consumes too much fat, there is no reason to try and cut it out of your diet altogether. Fat is an important nutrient for health – it protects our organs, allows women to sustain pregnancy and helps keep us warm. Some vitamins – A, D, E and K – are dependent on the presence of fat in order to be broken down and used within the body. Go too low and you won't be doing yourself any favours.

Fuelling your walking workouts

You already know that carbohydrate is the prime source of energy for working muscles, but when do you need to eat it, what type is best and how much do you need to fuel your walks?

You often hear that exercising on an empty stomach burns more fat. Well, it does. But it also feels harder, as the body is far less efficient at burning fat. So there's a trade-off – if you can work for longer because you have had something to eat and feel more energised, you'll ultimately burn more fat than if you struggle on with a grumbling tummy!

Ideally, you should eat 2–3 hours before your walk so that you have plenty of readily available energy. What should you eat? Make sure you have a carbohydrate-based meal with some protein. So a baked potato with tuna or cottage cheese, a poached egg on whole-grain toast, or cereal with milk and banana are all good options.

If you are embarking on a day's hike, or a long-distance walking session or event, you will need to factor in some refuelling along the way. It is best to pack small snacks to eat little and often, rather than a big lunch that will leave you feeling heavy and drowsy in the afternoon. Good choices include dried fruit, bananas, bagels, energy bars, peanut butter sandwiches, juice and yoghurt.

Staying hydrated

Even someone who barely stirs from the sofa still needs approximately 2500 ml of fluid a day for optimal functioning. Almost a third of this is derived from solid food. The rest comes from the fluids we consume, including water, juice, soft drinks, coffee and tea.

When you are exercising regularly, however, you need to drink more, in order to replace fluid lost through sweating. Studies have shown that we lose 500–1500 ml of fluid per hour of exercise, and a level of just 2 per cent dehydration can cause a decline in performance. Dehydration also causes heart rate to go up, increases 'stickiness' of the blood and makes exercise feel harder than it should.

Even if you never feel thirsty while exercising, trust the experts and try to take more fluid on board. You should think about hydrating yourself not just five minutes before you set off but throughout the day. Train yourself to drink more by sipping regularly, rather than gulping down loads at once, which may leave you feeling uncomfortable and bloated. It doesn't have to be water, but it's a good idea to consume at least half of your daily fluid as plain old water, as it is sugar-, caffeine- and calorie-free, and healthy.

If you are walking for a couple of hours or more, you may want to drink an isotonic sports drink instead of water, which will top up your carbohydrate stores as well as hydrate you. These also contain electrolyte salts, which replace sodium and potassium lost through sweating.

How much to glug?

Before you set off: consume 250–500 ml of fluid 15–30 minutes before your walk. It doesn't have to be all in one go – aim to consume this in the 30–60 minutes beforehand.

During your walk: aim to drink 100–250 ml every 15–20 minutes, depending on how hard you are exercising, the ambient temperature and your customary drinking and thirst.

Afterwards: After a tough session, you may want to rehydrate with a sports drink, or a carbohydrate-rich fluid such as orange juice or fruit-flavoured squash. But be wary of taking on extra calories from sports drinks if you are aiming to lose weight. Regardless of how long or intense your session was, you should drink at least half a litre of fluid afterwards. If you exercised for an hour or more, aim for a litre and keep drinking regularly for the next few hours until your urine is the colour of pale straw or lighter.

Get your vitamins and minerals

We only need them in tiny amounts, but vitamins and minerals each have a vital role to play in maintaining our health and, with the exception of vitamin D which can be derived from sunlight, must come from what we eat and drink. Providing your diet is healthy, balanced and varied, you will get sufficient quantities of all these essential micronutrients from your daily eating, but if you rely on pre-packaged and processed foods, or fail to consume a wide range of fruits, vegetables, whole grains and dairy products, it is possible that you are lacking. If this is the case, you may want to consider taking a good-quality multivitamin and mineral supplement.

According to recent research, the average adult in the UK eats around three portions of fruit and veg per day. The recommended figure is five, but this is considered a minimum rather than an ideal – evidence suggests that the phyto-chemicals, fibre, vitamins and minerals they contain make fruit and veg essential for fighting diseases such as cancer, heart disease, cataracts and osteoporosis. Try to eat as wide a variety of different types each day – go for different colours and textures to maximise the spread of nutrients.`

Let's walk

A high intake of saturated fat is linked to a high level of cholesterol. In turn, there is a link between the level of cholesterol in the blood and heart disease risk. But even more important is the ratio of good HDL cholesterol to bad LDL cholesterol. LDL is responsible in part for 'atherosclerosis,' the furring of the arteries that can cause heart attacks, because it travels to the lining of the coronary arteries where it can combine with oxygen and accelerate the development of scab-like plaques. But it seems that regular activity can help reduce LDL levels. Simultaneously, exercise – particularly more vigorous aerobic activities – can help to increase HDL cholesterol, whose role is to pick up cholesterol from the arteries and transport it to the liver to be broken down. In one study, subjects were assigned to participate in one of three walking programs. Each lasted for 24 weeks and involved a different walking pace. By the end of the trial, those on all three programs had substantially higher HDL levels than a control group who remained sedentary.

9 Special considerations

One of the great things about walking is that it is accessible and achievable for anyone – but there are a few groups for whom some additional points are worth bearing in mind to minimise the dangers and maximise enjoyment and performancesome of the best ways to walk

Walking and pregnancy

In its statement on pregnancy and exercise in 2002, the American College of Obstetrics and Gynaecology wrote: 'generally, participation in a wide range of recreational activities appears to be safe during pregnancy… In the absence of either medical or obstetric complications, 30 minutes or more of moderate exercise a day on most, if not all, days of the week is recommended for pregnant women.'

And the good news is, walking is one of the best activities you *can* do. It is low-impact, so it won't put additional stress on the joints and it is easily controllable and adaptable to suit your changing needs as your pregnancy progresses. It also helps boost circulation in the legs – reducing ankle swelling and the risk of developing varicose veins.

If you are already active when you become pregnant, the golden rule is to aim to maintain rather than improve your fitness level. Your body has enough to contend with, without you trying to crack the 12-minute mile! If you are pregnant and not currently active, then you need to approach embarking on activity more cautiously and talk to your doctor about what you plan to do.

There are a few conditions in which walking for fitness may not be advisable:

- If you are pregnant with twins or multiples.
- Previous premature births.
- High blood pressure.
- Bleeding during pregnancy.
- Extreme swelling of hands or feet.

What are the risks?

The three main concerns about exercising during pregnancy are foetal hypoxia (lack of oxygen), foetal hypoglycaemia (a lack of glucose) and a potentially hazardous rise in foetal temperature. But in humans, there is no evidence that moderate exercise causes such effects, at least not to an extent that could be detrimental to the growing baby.

For example, while there may be a reduction in blood flow to the uterus, caused by blood being redistributed to the working muscles, there have been no reported cases of foetal hypoxia resulting from exercise. Similarly, while increased carbohydrate metabolism in the muscles could be associated with a reduced glucose delivery to the baby, evidence suggests that pregnant women instinctively reduce the intensity and duration of their workouts to a level that doesn't deplete carbohydrate stores.

Regarding the final factor, research has not found any instances in which maternal temperature has been found to lead to foetal abnormalities in humans. But obviously, avoiding exercise in humid or hot weather or in a warm, stuffy indoor environment, as well as avoiding overly long exercise sessions, will minimise the risk. Staying well hydrated is even more important during pregnancy than normal – since blood volume has increased you need more fluid, regardless of whether or not you are exercising.

Walking for two in safety

- Inform your doctor of what you plan to do and ask whether they have any reason to advise you otherwise.

- Do not set goals or attempt to improve your fitness level – think maintenance.

- Exercise at conversation pace only – avoid overly high intensity exercise.

- Always warm up and cool down thoroughly.

- Stay well hydrated and exercise in cool temperatures. Studies show that while women instinctively keep up calorie intake during pregnancy, they often skimp on fluids and end up dehydrated.

- Avoid supine exercise (lying on your back) and stretches after the first trimester.

- Don't walk too far from home, or a reliable source of help and support, just in case you should start to feel unwell or something should happen.

- Consider wearing a maternity belt – or even a pair of Lycra cycle shorts to add support to your bump.

Walking through the menopause

Most women experience the menopause between the ages of 45 and 55 – the average is 52 years old. It is accompanied by a significant drop in female hormone levels – progesterone and oestrogen – and it is this that causes the classic symptoms of menopause – hot flushes, vaginal dryness, and most importantly bone loss. A reduction in bone density is the cause of osteoporosis, the disease that affects 1 in 3 women post-menopause, leading to frailty, loss of height and fractures. While the evidence is conflicting on how beneficial walking is in preserving bone density, it is certainly better than non-weight bearing activities such as swimming or cycling and will help to stave off age-related bone loss. See *Are you at risk?* on the next page.

Another health benefit of oestrogen that women lose post-menopause is its protective effect on the heart. While coronary heart disease is less of a risk for women than men under the age of 50, at menopause, the risk equals out for both sexes. Regular walking, as you know, significantly reduces this risk. Remaining – or even starting to be – active, as you now know, goes a long way towards maximising your chances of a healthy, longer life. It also seems that active women suffer less adverse effects of menopause – including weight gain, memory lapses and mood swings.

Are you at risk from osteoporosis?

These are some of the risk factors for osteoporosis. If you think you may be a likely candidate, ask your doctor for a DXA bone scan. Medication can prevent the loss of further bone, while an appropriate nutrition and exercise plan will also go some way towards preserving bone health.

- Being female.
- Early menopause or hysterectomy (before age 45).
- Slight build.
- Family history of the disease.
- Regular use of corticosteroid or anticoagulant drugs.
- Low lifelong level of weight-bearing physical activity.
- Low calcium intake.
- A period of amenorrhea (3 months or more without periods) or an eating disorder.
- Excessive yo-yo dieting or restricted calorie intake.
- Excessive alcohol or caffeine intake.
- Smoking.
- Race – Caucasians are more at risk than Afro-Caribbean or Asian races.

Walking in later life

Whether you are just beginning or have been active for years, the benefits of walking regularly as you get older are undisputed. Research from the University of Michigan suggests that being active in your 50s and 60s reduces the risk of premature death. Based on over 9000 adults, the research found that active seniors were 35 per cent less likely to die in the following 8 years compared to sedentary people.

Let's walk

Walking is great for everybody – young or old, small or large, male or female, but there are some specific benefits that women can reap as they progress through life's hormonal changes. Research published in the *Journal of Psychomatic Research* found that three months of regular exercise dampened pre-menstrual symptoms – especially mood-related ones – while active women report less period pain and pre-menstrual syndrome than sedentary ones. You might also find that upping your activity level boosts your sex drive, too. An American study found that out of 8000 women aged 18–49, those who exercised at least three times a week reported greater arousal, more frequent sex and more frequent orgasm than sedentary women. Women who exercise during pregnancy are less liable to suffer irritations such as heart burn, swelling of the extremities, constipation and poor sleep. But more importantly, they also lower their risk of suffering gestational diabetes or pre-eclampsia, and tend to have higher birth weight babies, who are less prone to early-life health problems. Burning 1000 calories through exercise per week increases baby birth weight by 5 per cent.

Meanwhile, research published in 2004 in the *Journal of the American Medical Association* found that elderly men who walked less than a quarter of a mile per day were nearly twice as likely (a 1.8 fold increased risk) to develop dementia and Alzheimer's disease compared to men who walk more than 2 miles per day. Earlier research, from the University of Illinois, found that when over-60s who were sedentary took up walking 3 days a week for 45 minutes, their mental processing ability improved. Concentration, reaction time and multi-tasking all improved in the adults who began walking who were aged 60–75. What's more, their walking speed increased to an average of 16 minutes per mile over the six months of the study. Finally, Oregon Health Sciences University found that starting a walking program lowered the intraocular pressure of 40 sedentary individuals, which decreased their risk of glaucoma. You can read more about the health benefits of walking in chapter 1 – and rest assured that these are rewards that it is never too late to earn.

The only caveat worth mentioning is that it can take longer to see improvements, due to age-related declines in the cardiovascular and musculoskeletal systems, and a reduction in the levels of many hormones involved in cell growth and renewal, such as human growth hormone. So be patient!

As far as nutrition goes, the same basic rules apply to older walkers as to everyone else. But it's very important to get sufficient calcium – post-menopausal women need 1000 mg, while men need 800 mg. This is because calcium is a key nutrient in the maintenance of bone density, which declines as we age and may increase the risk of osteoporosis, the bone thinning disease that leads to frailty, loss of height and a high risk of fractures. Women are particularly vulnerable post menopause, as plummeting oestrogen levels can cause as much as 2–5 per cent bone loss per year in the five years following the cessation of periods. If you take a supplement, look for calcium carbonate with vitamin D (which aids absorption) as more of the calcium is 'available' than from other forms

Wiser walking

- Warm up and cool down for longer – older joints and muscles take longer to get moving!
- Drink plenty of fluids. In one study, active healthy men aged 67–75 were less thirsty and drank less voluntarily after being water-deprived than did younger men.
- Be more vigilant about exercising in extreme heat or cold. As we age, we get more prone to dehydration and heatstroke, while very cold weather causes the blood vessels to constrict, putting extra strain on the heart. Dress appropriately for the conditions.
- Allow yourself longer to recover between sessions.
- Stretch vigilantly. Muscles and connective tissues begin to lose their elasticity as we age, making flexibility work an essential part of your regime.

Pace matters

An interesting study suggests that the pace at which older people walk determines the health benefits reaped. A group of post-menopausal women, ages 50-65, who were in good health but sedentary, were put on a programme in which they walked three miles a day for a total of 15 miles a week for eight months. Insulin and growth hormone (GH) levels were measured at the beginning, mid-point and end of the study along with body fat and total weight. Those who walked at a slower (18-20 minute mile) pace became more insulin-sensitive - good news for those at risk for diabetes. But sensitivity to insulin tapered off as walking speed increased. However, the brisk (15-minute mile pace) walkers secreted more growth hormone, which promotes bone and tissue formation and helps reduce the effects of aging. GH secretion is known to decline with age

The brisk walkers lost slightly more weight overall than the slower walkers but the difference was minimal. The bottom line? Mix up your walks to include faster and slower-paced efforts.

Resources and further information

Walking organisations

The British Walking Federation

Organises non-competitive walking events of 3–26 miles, designed for people of all ages and abilities.
BWF National Office:
112 Crescent Road, Reading
Berks, RG1 5SW
www.bwf-ivv.org.uk

The Long Distance Walkers' Association

Promotes long-distance walking in the UK countryside and requires membership. LDWA Membership Secretary:
4 Chestnut Way, Formby
Merseyside L37 2DP
www.ldwa.org.uk

Nordic Walking

Qualified instructors and regular classes, advice on technique and purchasing poles.
Nordic Health:
Tel. 020 8211 3512
www.nordicwalking.co.uk

The Race Walking Association

The UK governing body for race walking. Send for a free introductory pack to learn more about the sport or visit the website to find out if there is a local club near you.
Race Walking Association:
Tel. 01277 220687
www.racewalkingassocation.btinternet.co.uk

The Ramblers' Association

Advice and information on getting the most out of walking in Britain, with regular guided group walks, suggested routes, a forum for walkers and holidays.
Rambler's Association:
Tel. 020 7339 8500
www.ramblers.org.uk

Walking the Way to Health

A joint partnership between the British Heart Foundation and the Countryside Agency, aiming to increase physical activity and improve the health of the nation. The site has a walk finder, lists of walking events, details of walking groups nationwide as well as 'green gyms' – outdoor conservation/gardening work with a physical focus.
The Countryside Agency:
Tel. 01242 533258
www.whi.org.uk

Walking World

Britain's largest online walking guide. Every walk comes with an easy-to-follow photographic guide and an Ordnance Survey map.
Walkingworld Ltd:
Tel. 0117 952 1628
www.walkingworld.com

YMCA Fitness Industry Training
Offers courses to teach walking for fitness.
Tel. 020 7343 1850
www.ymcafit.org.uk

Walking events

The Playtex MoonWalk
It takes place in June each year and is the world's only power-walking marathon and takes place in London at night! Entries go quickly so register well before the deadline!
Tel. 01483 741 430
www.walkthewalk.org

Race for Life
An annual series of national 5 km events for women walking, jogging or running in aid of Cancer Research UK.
Tel. 08705 134 314
www.raceforlife.org

Walk for Life
An annual 10 km sponsored walk through central London for HIV and AIDS.
Tel. 0870 787 5348
www.walkforlife.co.uk

Walk the Walk
Encourages people to take part in walking events and races to raise money for breast cancer research, cancer care and to become fitter and healthier.
www.walkthewalk.org

Walking holidays and breaks

Charity Challenge
Organises over 100 'responsible tourism' expeditions each year worldwide (not all walking) all in aid of fundraising for various charities.
Tel. 020 8557 0000
www.charitychallenge.com

Exodus
Walking holidays that are about the place you visit as much as the walking itself.
Tel. 0870 240 5550
www.exodus.co.uk

HF Holidays
Walking holidays in the UK, Europe and worldwide.
Tel. 020 8511 1525
www.hfholidays.co.uk

Inntravel
Independent walking holiday specialists. Walks are generally self-guided with detailed notes and maps. Luggage transported.
Tel. 01653 617788
www.inntravel.co.uk

Ramblers' Holidays
Sister organisation to the Ramblers' Association, offering walking holidays globally. Also offers UK short break holidays through affiliate Countrywide Holidays:
Tel. 01707 331133
www.ramblersholidays.co.uk
www.countrywidewalking.com

WalkingWomen
Women's walking holidays across the UK and abroad – many women go solo.
Tel. 08456 445335
www.walkingwomen.com

Waymark Holidays
Organised walking holidays in Europe – specialising in areas that are off the beaten track. Small group sizes and graded levels of difficulty.
Tel. 01753 516 477
www.waymarkholidays.com

Footwear, clothing and accessories

Adidas
www.adidas.co.uk

The Adventure Shop
Online store selling numerous brands, clothing, accessories and gadgets.
www.adventureshop.co.uk

Berghaus
www.berghaus.co.uk

Brasher
Footwear and accessories including trekking poles.
www.brasher.co.uk

Less Bounce
Sports bra specialist.
Tel. 08000 363840
www.lessbounce.com

Lowe Alpine
Clothing and accessories only.
Tel. 01539 740840
www.lowealpine.co.uk

Merrell
Footwear only.
www.merrellboot.com

New Balance
Clothing and footwear.
www.newbalance.co.uk

Nike
www.nike.com

The North Face
Clothing, accessories and footwear.
www.thenorthface.com/eu

Odlo
Clothing and sports underwear.
www.odlo.com

Rohan
Clothing and accessories.
www.rohan.co.uk

1000 Mile Sportswear
Socks and accessories.
www.1000mile.co.uk

Gadgets and accessories

4My Way of Life
Gadgets, heart rate monitors and injury prevention equipment
Tel. 0870 241 5471
www.4mywayoflife.com

Garmin
Global positioning systems.
01794 519944
www.garmin.co.uk

ICON Health & Fitness
Treadmills and home exercise gear.
Tel. 0113 387 7122
www.nordic-track.com/uk

Leki
Trekking and Nordic Walking poles.
www.leki.com

Life Fitness
Treadmills and home exercise gear.
Tel. 01353 665507
www.lifefitness.com

Ordnance Survey
Mapping and map sales.
Tel. www.ordnancesurvey.co.uk

Pedometers.co.uk
Pedometers, compasses, map measurers and other walking accessories online.
Tel. 01327 706030
www.pedometers.co.uk

Polar
Heart rate monitors.
Tel. 01926 816177
www.polar-uk.com

Salomon
Bags and bumbelts.
Tel. 0800 389 4350
www.salomonsports.com

Injury prevention and body maintenance

British Chiropractic Association
To find a qualified registered chiropractor in your area:
Tel. 0118 950 5950
www.chiropractic-uk.co.uk

Chartered Society of Physiotherapy
To find a chartered physiotherapist:
www.csp.org.uk

National Register of Personal Trainers
By searching this national database of qualified, experienced personal trainers you should be able to find one with a special interest in walking
www.nrpt.org.uk

Society of Chiropodists and Podiatrists
To find a local practitioner:
tel. 020 7234 8620
www.feetforlife.org

Sports Massage Association
To find an accredited sports massage practitioner:
SMA, PO Box 44347, London SW19 1WD. Tel. 020 8545 0861
www.sportsmassageassociation.org

Index